Work Matters

GW00777287

Work is complicated: it can be fulfilling and exciting, or disappointing and disruptive. We spend most of our adult lives at work; it shapes our identities and provides a context for our creativity and talents. It can be the source of great pleasure – and of profound distress.

In *Work Matters*, organizational consultant and Tavistock lecturer Francesca Cardona examines our changing relationship with work today. Drawing on case studies from a wide range of individuals and organizations, she considers the dynamics at play in our working lives. Cardona examines how to navigate times of transition, and the balance of power in the work place, while also addressing latent issues such as the effects of shame, the cost of ill-conceived organizational structures and tasks, the interface between the personal and the professional, and the manager's most precious skill: the ability to be psychologically present. Finally, Cardona casts an eye on the consultant's role in helping organizations move forwards in ways that are professionally and personally rewarding.

Whether you are a business leader, manager, consultant or student, or simply interested in how your work affects you, *Work Matters* offers essential insights into an area that occupies so much of our lives.

Francesca Cardona is an organizational consultant and teacher of consultancy and coaching in the Tavistock tradition. Italian by birth, she has been based in London since the mid-eighties. She works in a variety of organizational and cultural contexts, helping leaders and organizations to face issues of change, transition and the emotional dimension of organizational life.

Work Matters

Consulting to Leaders and Organizations
in the Tavistock Tradition

Francesca Cardona

LONDON AND NEW YORK

First published 2020
by Routledge
2 Park Square, Milton Park, Abingdon, Oxon OX14 4RN

and by Routledge
52 Vanderbilt Avenue, New York, NY 10017

Routledge is an imprint of the Taylor & Francis Group, an informa business

British Library Cataloguing-in-Publication Data
A catalogue record for this book is available from the British Library

Library of Congress Cataloging-in-Publication Data
A catalog record has been requested for this book

ISBN: 978-0-367-31317-3 (hbk)
ISBN: 978-0-367-31318-0 (pbk)
ISBN: 978-0-429-31743-9 (ebk)

Typeset in Bembo
by Wearset Ltd, Boldon, Tyne and Wear

To Gennaro, Luca and Marco

Contents

PART III
The consultant's role: an anthropologist at work   81

    negotiating a contract with a new client   83

9   The consultancy stage: the 'third' dimension in the
    engagement between client and consultant   89

10 Who is the boss? Balancing power and vulnerability in the
    client–consultant relationship   97

11 Ending and regeneration: reflections on the emotional
    experience of ending a consultancy assignment   104

    Conclusion   114

    Bibliography   116
    Index   122

Foreword

Looking at the coaching and consultancy field from a publications perspective, there has been a clear change as the market has grown enormously over the past five years. Coaching and consultancy of various sorts have of late become increasingly 'fashionable' and the topic nowadays draws individuals from neighbouring professions, such as psychiatrists, psychotherapists, counsellors, HR personnel and even sectors such as banking.

Yet the main suppliers of the 'coaching and leadership' commodity consists of a handful of global consultants. For the average reader their works are beyond application. And while many other individual consultants' writings and publications can be impressive, too often they give details only of specific areas of work. For the leader, manager and consultant these can be hard to apply to their own situations.

Francesca and her new book fit into neither of the above mentioned categories, and are therefore a most welcome addition to the field. Her book is ripe with experiences of coaching and consultancy, with the exceptional advantage that what comes out of it is easily understandable and therefore applicable to tasks that the reader might have in their in-tray.

Her thoughtfulness, experience and expertise arise from the fact she has had numerous engagements across the whole spectrum of consulting, coaching and leadership, and has made excellent use of reflecting on the learning to be had. Like the master craftsmen and women of the past (think of the painter Angelica Kauffman) she has had placements in a variety of settings throughout her native Italy and elsewhere in Europe, and many years to take in and take on the English field of work.

One of the pitfalls of training in the coaching/consultancy field is that one can become an acolyte of the 'grand master or mistress' at whose feet one sits. Given the widespread work she has done, Francesca has avoided this trap and instead offers a mix and match of possible interventions that enable the reader to find their own style.

Her book is a rich and enriching collection of techniques and interventions. Newcomers to the field should have a copy and it would do old–timers no harm whatsoever to have a copy by their bedside as a sample of how reflection and learning can be integrated into one's life's work.

Anton Obholzer

Acknowledgements

I am grateful for the ideas and insights that emerged from discussions with students of the Tavistock programmes I have taught on and convened, and for all of the dialogues shared with close colleagues inside and outside Tavistock Consulting. I am indebted to all of them for their thoughts and comments over the years.

More specifically I wish to thank all of the people who have encouraged and supported me on the journey of writing this book.

First of all, my editor and 'partner in crime': Sue Lascelles. Her professionalism, 'outsider' perspective and warm encouragement provided me with much needed structure, focus and support.

I would like to extend this thank you to my first readers, Megan Meredith and Derek Raffaelli, whose comments and feedback have been invaluable in refining the contents of this book.

And to my sons, Luca and Marco, for their enthusiasm for this endeavour, with a special thank you to Luca for his wonderful design of the cover.

I also wish to express my gratitude to my mentors, Franca Manoukian, Eric Miller, Harold Bridger and Anton Obholzer. Their innovative thinking, insights and pioneering practices have been, and remain, a constant inspiration.

A note on confidentiality

All names of the examples in the book are fictitious and the identifying details have been changed to preserve anonymity.

Several case illustrations are composite descriptions of individuals and organizations presenting similar dynamics.

Introduction

Why this book?

Love and work are the cornerstones of our humanness.

Sigmund Freud

Work, like love, is complicated. It can be fulfilling and exciting as well as disappointing and disruptive.

Work is 'life': it shapes our identity and gives us a setting in which to exercise our creativity and competence. It can be the source of both great pleasure and profound distress.

Work is challenging, regardless of people's experience and commitment.

I have always been interested in the world of work. From early on, I expected to enter a profession: I was both excited and daunted by the prospect of engaging with work. While my initial experiences were disappointing, they provided me with significant learning opportunities. As I will explain below, different elements ultimately contributed to my choice of career; however, I realize now that my struggle at a very demanding and rigid high school was probably my strongest initial motivation: it generated my desire to 'do something' about organizational dysfunction and individual stress.

My personal sense of being both an outsider and an insider, the political context of my formative years, my own experience of organizational distress and the encounter with psychoanalysis had a profound influence on my career and approach to work. The outsider–insider dynamic remains central to my choice of profession: it is a very familiar experience, a space where I feel at home.

Brought up in Genoa, a proud and reticent provincial town in Italy, and coming from a family of diverse outsiders – grandparents from Umbria, Emilia Romagna, Dalmatia and Great Britain – I learnt to move in and out, to observe and join in, wanting to belong as well as feeling different. I learnt to manage the tension between taking part and staying outside, looking in from an outside position, while also experiencing empathy for, and curiosity about, other people's situations and dilemmas.

I was at university in the seventies, a period of great turmoil, idealism and determination to change society. Though at times naïve and removed from reality, my generation looked for professions where we could make a difference. In one of my first jobs, as a therapist for deaf children, I experienced the negative impact of an ill-conceived service and role. It was a painful job for a young woman at the beginning of her career; being part of an organization with a very poor structure, lack of a clear purpose and little emotional and professional support. However, thanks to the help of my first mentor, Franca Manoukian, and a subsequent training in group and organizational dynamics, I began to make sense of my experience and developed a strong interest in this field. In parallel, I started a psychoanalytic journey that I continued when I moved to London.

I was very fortunate to join the Tavistock Institute of Human Relations (TIHR) in the mid-eighties, as a Fellow of a programme on consultancy and organizations, where I met Eric Miller and Harold Bridger, both great inspirations and wonderful mentors. While doing my training at TIHR I joined the 'Consultancy to Institutions Workshop' led by Anton Obholzer at the Tavistock Clinic, where I was a member for almost 20 years. The Workshop produced *The Unconscious at Work*, a book now regarded as a 'classic' in our field (a second edition was published in 2019). I grew up professionally in that environment, and met many colleagues who are still a strong influence on my work.

Being a member of the Workshop, combined with the teaching on the Tavistock Master Course on Organizational Consultancy, gave me a professional context and identity, and the experience of being part of an inspiring and exciting professional 'tribe'. It was during those years that the system-psychodynamic approach was developed as a more clearly defined method for understanding and consulting to organizations, building on the work of Eric Miller, A. K. Rice and others at the TIHR.

This book is generated from that background.

Organizational consultancy

Because of the instability and turbulence that exist in the work place today, organizations can no longer provide for the dependency needs of their employees, and are facing new and diverse challenges. Leaders have to rely increasingly on their capacity to adapt to a changing environment, be psychologically present and provide leadership that is both consultative and emotionally tuned in to their workforce. In this respect, organizational consultancy and coaching can provide a valuable 'space for work': consultancy offers the opportunity to step back, pause and gain a different perspective. It can help individuals and organizations become more reflective, resilient and open to change and transformation.

Gaining insights into our motivations and desires, making a connection between our engagement with work and the primary goals of the organization, and understanding the underlying dynamics in the work environment lie at the core of my own consultancy work.

The consultant's role is both exciting and frightening. There is the desire to create a productive partnership with the client, as well as the anxiety of potentially having a sterile encounter. Both clients and consultants can experience the exhilaration of embracing new possibilities and the dread of leaving familiar places (a theme that will be explored in Chapter 10).

A lot of my work with leaders and teams happens *back stage*. As organizational consultants, we rarely have an opportunity, beyond our network, to share our understanding of the work environment, our impact on organizational development and our own experience as consultants. Our work is often invisible.

As a lecturer in organizational consultancy, I have presented and discussed my ideas, conceptual framework and consultancy experience with many generations of students. This book is an attempt to speak to an even wider group. The intention is to contribute to the development of this relatively new area of intervention, still in some respects regarded as being more of a craft than a fully fledged profession. The focus of this book is therefore on the practice of organizational consultancy rather than on its academic side.

With this book, I want to reach out to people in work, both outside and inside organizations, and to offer a framework for understanding their experiences. The stories I share are designed to help readers deepen their insights into the dynamics at play in their own working lives.

This book is also for my fellow consultants who are working in the Tavistock tradition or who take a different approach. It will be an opportunity for them to revisit their professional journey and compare, identify and disagree with what I make of mine.

The contents and structure of this book

In Part I, I talk about the context and meaning of work in '*The context of work: A love affair in the changing world*', discussing the exciting opportunities that work offers, as well as its sense of uncertainty and instability. The section '*Ambivalent love*' explores women's relationship to work and the 'ambivalent love' they often experience in relation to it, as a result of the conflicting demands of raising a family.

In the introduction to Part II, I discuss the 'system–psychodynamic' approach – and provide a map of the key concepts underpinning my practice. The following chapters then describe different organizational and leadership dynamics through many examples drawn from my consultancy practice.

Chapter 1: The team as a sponge describes how seemingly similar individuals and groups can behave in extremely diverse ways when working with different client groups. The term 'sponge' describes the striking way in which the team absorbs the central dynamics which operate within its client group.

Chapter 2: Vulnerable leadership focuses on a specific phase of a consultancy project, when the director of an organization became terminally ill. It describes how, when a personal tragedy strikes, any negotiated boundaries seem to collapse and how this can affect the life of an organization.

Chapter 3: Organizational and personal shame describes how three individuals responded to powerful experiences of shame in their working lives, and how consultancy helped them to regain a sense of confidence and competence.

Chapter 4: The grey area, consulting at the interface between the personal and the professional, illustrates how the capacity to understand the link between current difficulties in a leadership role and early life experiences can have a trans-formative effect and generate shifts in behaviour and organizational dynamics.

Chapter 5: The challenge of succession portrays a number of consultancy assignments focused on succession, and how the old and new generations have dealt with the process of endings and new beginnings.

Chapter 6: The manager's most precious skill describes how in a context of constant organizational change, the manager's capacity to be fully present becomes an essential element for stability and growth.

Chapter 7: Consulting to the boss looks at leadership beyond the textbooks and the experience of a number of leaders, along with the factors that have helped them to sustain and develop their roles at an individual and organizational level.

Part III, *The consultant's role: an anthropologist at work,* describes the role and dilemmas of the organizational consultant working within the approach of the Tavistock tradition. It explores the challenges of engaging with complex client systems, the risk of collusion, the dynamic of entering and ending a consultancy project, and the balance of power between consultant and client.

Chapter 8: The complexity of entry draws on a number of different examples to describe how the initial engagement with the client can provide key data for understanding the underlying organizational dynamics and issues.

Chapter 9: The consultancy stage describes how physical spaces have a powerful role in enhancing, inhibiting and developing psychological work, and can strongly influence the consultancy engagement.

Chapter 10: Who is the boss? is about balancing power and vulnerability in the client–consultant relationship, the complexity of this relationship and the need for constant adjustment, mutual challenge and review.

Chapter 11: Ending and regeneration offers reflections on the emotional experience of ending a consultancy assignment, closing a contract and termi-nating a working relationship.

Conclusion provides some reflections on the writing journey and on the author's challenge to convey key ideas to the readership in her mind

Our experience of work is influenced by what we bring to it – our desires, expectations and anxieties, by the demands of the task, and by the dynamics of the organizational culture and the wider environment. The way we navigate work is shaped by our capacity to engage with its complexity, by our awareness of what is at play and our ability to have some influence and agency in our organizational context. (I will explore this theme in Part I.)

The stories I tell are based on real clients, although I have changed many details to preserve confidentiality. Several vignettes are a mixture of different situations, which presented very similar dynamics.

I feel privileged I have been 'allowed in' by many individuals and teams, who have shared their concerns and difficulties as well as their desires and plans with me. This book is also for them: if they think they recognize themselves in any of the stories I tell, I hope they feel 'represented' fairly – with interest, compassion and a critical stance.

Part I

The context of work

A love affair – the meaning of work in a changing world

As an organizational consultant, my main focus is on the nature of people's engagement with work, in the understanding that work is central to their lives and could be a source of great pleasure as well as of great distress. In the current complex and uncertain environment, work could be compared to a love affair, one that offers exciting opportunities, adventures and challenges, but also a profound sense of uncertainty and instability. Work as 'a love affair' brings passion and desire as well as turbulence, disappointment and despair.

Our interest and focus can be affected by a lack of connection or an ambivalent attachment to our work place and by the experience of not been sufficiently 'held' by our organizational environment; the notion of being 'held' is linked to Winnicott's idea of the 'holding environment' the mother provides for her baby, a secure place for his development and emotional growth (Winnicott, 1971).

As in a love affair, we might feel frustrated with respect to our expectations around a sense of belonging, stability and long-term commitment. On the other hand, we can also learn how to navigate this fluid environment and create opportunities for ourselves that are more tuned in and connected to the changing environment itself. This requires a capacity to be open and to tolerate the anxiety of inhabiting a '*fluid zone*' without looking too hard for defined answers and certainty, shifting our perception and expectations of the work paradigm.

Fluidity, or liquidity, has become a metaphor of the present phase in the history of modernity (Bauman, 2000). Instability and flexibility are now the norm. Organizations are always in flow, in endless *becoming*. Today, work, both in practice and in our minds, has loose shapes, permeable boundaries and is often unpredictable – a changeable network of relationships, roles, multiple identities and groups.

Freud, when talking of love and work, spoke of 'a general work productiveness which would not preoccupy the individual to the extent that his right or capacity to be a sexual and loving being would be lost' (Erikson, 1959, quoting Freud). Yet work is now at the centre of our personas; it is increasingly becoming part of our core identity because of its containing function and because our experience of being part of an organization is disappearing (Cooper and Dartington, 2004).

Alain de Botton argues that our choice of occupation defines our identity 'to the extent that the most insistent question we ask of new acquaintances is not where they come from or who their parents were, but what they do' (2009, p. 106). In a fast-changing world, where organizations are less containing and technological innovations increase opportunities for virtual relationships, the issue of our work identity becomes even more central. Our work identity is related much more closely to the competencies we can exercise in different settings, real and virtual, than to an organization. The boundaries between work identity and personal identity are becoming more flexible (Cooper and Dartington, 2004).

The concept of the organization as the 'container' and work as the contained has been challenged. Work becomes the main container for our emotional investment and could be experienced as a malignant as well as an idealized container. Many of my clients have felt at some point in their careers a sense of persecution from their work, while also idealizing the potentials of their role and situation (see also Part II on containment).

Work represents our capacity to invest in something away from our own immediate surroundings, a 'third dimension' beyond our individuality, family and community. However, the nature of our *attachment* to work is related to the diminishing organizational containment in organizations. As Bowlby points out, attachment is a 'primary motivational system' starting in infancy and operating throughout our lives (Bowlby, 1973). Our capacity for attachment to work and organizational life is also inevitably linked to our early experience of emotional attachment. Without some degree of attachment to a meaningful activity, work can start to feel superfluous and can affect our capacity to feel fulfilled.

Ambivalent work attachment

Miles, a bright and ambitious manager in a large global company, has progressed to a senior role that he finds interesting and challenging. However, his ability to take pleasure in what he does is limited. He arrives at his coaching session looking tired after a very intense couple of weeks abroad. In a flat voice, he tells me how he organized a successful conference and that he will soon be promoted to a global role. I comment on how positive and exciting this sounds, though he seems unable to express any enjoyment about his achievements.

I connect this experience to his background. University and work have represented an escape from a complex family environment for him and a means to his independence. The absence of parental interest has made him deeply insecure about his worth. As a result, his investment in work, particularly at the beginning of his career, lacked emotional engagement. Even now, much more secure in his personal life, Miles struggles to feel fully attached to work, despite his commitment and success. The anxiety of engaging with a potentially 'negative container' often generates withdrawal and detachment in him. This experience is emphasized by an organization that operates a lot virtually and by a leadership team that is scattered around the world.

In the coaching sessions, we address Miles's problems around feelings of entitlement and his struggle to trust authority, so painfully connected with the experience of his distant parents. His efficiency, determination and focus seem at times to compensate for his sense of emptiness and his unfulfilled emotional needs. We also talk about his longing for 'attachment' and how he could develop a safe enough 'container' in his organizational context, despite the physical distance of his boss and some of his peers.

Ambivalent attachment towards organizations can also be linked to the growing culture of *performativity*, where the emphasis is on performance and results rather than loyalty and belonging: 'We become ontologically insecure: unsure whether we are doing enough, doing the right thing, doing as much as others, or as well as others, constantly looking to improve, to be better, to be excellent' (Ball, 2003, p. 220).

Hoggett, professor of social policy, talks of three dysfunctional elements in our current organizational environment: triumph of numbers, performativity and fragile narcissism. Numbers are mistaken as the 'real thing' – i.e. what can't be counted doesn't count – and there is a widespread feeling that nothing is ever good enough. He suggests that the anxiety raised by a culture of performativity leads us into 'survival mode' that prevents us from engaging with the meaning of what we do. He also links it with shame and feelings of failure, exposure and humiliation. Shame produces a sense of inferiority in a context where only the strong seem to survive and vulnerability is not accepted (Hoggett, 2016) – I will discuss the theme of shame in more detail in Chapter 3.

As Sennett says, 'Failure is the great modern taboo…. Coming to terms with failure may haunt us internally but seldom is discussed with others' (Sennett, 1998, p. 118).

Driven by performance anxiety

Victor was an engineer in a global company who attended a leadership development workshop that I facilitated. I knew, from the head of human resources, that my client group – senior executives with a technical background – were struggling to engage with the 'emotional side' of leadership and were quite reluctant to spend two full days of training in this area. After quite a difficult start, with many of the workshop members constantly gazing at their mobile phones, I suggested that they each attempt to draw their organization – a free, individual drawing representing the 'organization in their mind' (Armstrong, 2005).

Victor's drawing was of a huge plane that dominated the whole flip-chart paper; in a corner, three tiny figures represented his wife and children. Close to tears, he explained how he was hardly ever home and missed seeing his children growing up. One after the other, the members of the group then described a life of constant travel, away from their families, feeling compelled to reach very ambitious commercial targets.

Lucey talks of her experience of working with executives 'who are very caught up in a performance approach and, at the same time, seem to be longing for meaning that has been lost as a result of this approach' (Lucey, 2015, p. 215).

Applying Bick's concept of 'second skin defences' in infants to organizational life (Bick, 1968), she describes the pseudo-protective layers that individuals build up in response to failures of containment: 'Second skin-type functioning involves an adhesive form of identification which is a superficial way of relating, as opposed to the more in depth three-dimensional way characteristic of containing relationships' (p. 217). This second skin often represents a cover-up for underlying anxieties and the authentic experiences of the individuals. As a consequence, a performativity approach doesn't allow the development of a sense of purpose that gives authenticity to the experience or which allows people to take up their roles with accountability and authority (Bazalgette *et al.*, 2009, p. 9).

Work and creativity

Work also represents the diversion of aggression and sexuality: 'In work, as contrasted with purposeless destruction, the aggressive impulses are moulded and guided in a constructive direction by the influence of the creative (erotic) instinct …' (Menninger, 1942, p. 33). Our engagement with work is an expression of our creativity, but creativity also brings with it the anxiety surrounding our capacity to be disruptive. The drive to be creative comes from a feeling of lack; work can provide an outlet for filling this sense of emptiness.

Creativity can also disrupt our personal and organizational status quo. The creation of something new and different implies a loss – the loss of familiar relationships, patterns and structures – just as the birth of a child can bring with it a sense of loss and anxiety about what has been created. The capacity to manage the tension between our creativity and our anxiety about disruptiveness is essential for the development of a healthy engagement with our work and role.

Theresa, a social entrepreneur with huge energy and a great capacity for innovation, had just opened a new pioneering family centre after overcoming incredible bureaucratic obstacles from the local authorities. As soon as she started this challenging and exciting new venture she suddenly became distracted by many other projects and a number of commitments abroad.

With my help, she gradually began to realize how anxious she felt after the 'birth' of this new project, the product of her creativity and desire. Theresa wasn't afraid of the challenges ahead; she was anxious about engaging with something she had created that could become potentially disruptive or profoundly disappointing.

Creativity is connected with the concept of finding and generating meaning in order to feel fulfilled and engaged in what we do. The sense of meaning needs to be sustainable in order to allow us to manage and accept the contrasting feelings connected with the creative process. Armstrong talks of discovery or recovery of meaning, finding meaning and making meaning: 'Work needs always to be rooted in – or at least to provide space for – the evolution of meaning, which is necessarily provisional and transitional, but without which such terms risk a kind of emotional degeneration' (Armstrong 2005, p. 67).

Engaging with the love affair

Miles's experience of work became much worse after his boss left the company. The incoming new boss was based in another continent and had a very different approach. Much more directive and less facilitative, he didn't seem to have much time or space for Miles.

Miles was losing his confidence. His fear of work as a 'bad container' – linked to his early experience of family life – seemed to be confirmed. It took him a long time to be able to engage with his new work situation in a different way. He had to let go of his ideas about what 'should' happen and be more open to what the new boss had to offer so that an element of trust and collaboration could develop. He became gradually more able to 'hear' his boss and could share his views and plans for the future without feeling under scrutiny and as though he were in a risky position.

It is tempting at times to feel nostalgic about the past or overcritical about the present; wanting the present to be different, rather than engaging with what it is. However, if our aspirations are for consistency, stability and predictability, we live in the wrong era. That said, if we had lived at the time of the industrial revolution, a period of radical change in the world of work and society, we might have experienced similar feelings of confusion, uncertainty and instability – as well as excitement, curiosity and interest. Now, like then, a technological revolution is fundamentally altering the way we live, work and relate to one another.

Navigating the world of work today requires a capacity to create attachments and containing structures in a different way. This entails a shift in how we think about work and how we translate this understanding into our expectations and practice, with the acknowledgement that today's fluid organizational environment can increase our anxieties and our capacity to be present and fully engaged in our work.

The culture of performativity is difficult to resist or to manage. Driven by anxiety, often generated by scarce resources in the public sector or by a drive for profit in private companies, it represents a malaise of our times.

It is challenging for individuals, leaders and organizations to maintain a reflective stance that can help them to make sense of, and develop, a healthy sense of perspective on their working realities.

Forming attachments and being part of containing structures remain crucial for a healthy and meaningful involvement with work. The challenge is to learn how to do it – moving from the turbulence of a 'love affair' to a more stable relationship – without denying the unpredictability of the environment we are in.

Ambivalent love?

Women's relationship and relatedness to work

In the previous section I discussed work as a love affair, with respect to both the pleasure and pain that work entails. This section focuses on women's relationship to work and the 'ambivalent love' they often experience in relation to it, as a result of the conflicting demands of raising a family.

A few years ago, I offered consultation to a number of women with children who wanted to re-think the directions of their careers. Some were looking for a more fulfilling occupation; others were in very demanding jobs and wanted to find a more balanced approach to work and motherhood. They were all quite unhappy and stressed about their situations, either feeling unchallenged and frustrated in their jobs, or too strained and overwhelmed by the demands of their work roles.

I felt that beyond their individual circumstances – their family backgrounds, their personalities and surroundings – there was a common crucial dilemma at the core of the situation for these intelligent, capable and caring women: the expectation and pressure, from themselves and from society, that well educated women should have an interesting and rewarding career while being able to bring up a family.

I was struck by the amount of pain and distress they were experiencing in relation to both their longing for a meaningful job and the desire to spend quality time with their children during their children's early years of development. Despite their many differences, these women were all struggling to combine work and family. Their wish and need for financial independence and fulfilment were key elements in their search for a satisfying career. Raising a young family was experienced as something that was often difficult or impossible to combine with rewarding and ambitious jobs.

Yet I felt that despite the complexity of their individual situations and their feelings of being stuck, these women could still recover some sense of choice and agency.

Women and work is frequently the subject of articles and research in an era in which most women in the west are in the work place: 80 per cent of mothers now work outside the home and 25 per cent are in professional jobs.

Questions about the glass ceiling, the relatively small number of women in senior management positions, and of excellent academic qualifications not matching career successes have prompted a debate about how women engage with work and how their approach differs from men's.

Susan Pinker, in her book *The Sexual Paradox*, says: 'If you have to predict the future on the basis of school achievements the world would be a matriarchy.' In her many years of clinical experience, she has treated mostly boys:

> To my surprise I began to see many of my charges featured as success stories in the press.... Meanwhile, many of the girls their age who were light years ahead of them … opted for paths that would not necessarily lead them to the highest status or the most lucrative careers. They had other goals.
>
> (Pinker, 2008, p. 6)

The management and the tension between 'work' and 'family' remains a central dilemma for many women. Equal opportunities don't automatically bring equal results. The increasing equality and educational successes of many women have contributed to cover up the complexity of the issue. There is often a denial of the real dilemma between work and family, and of the gender difference in our attitudes towards these.

Work as 'internal object'

The concept of 'internal objects' comes from psychoanalysis, the idea that our inner world is populated by mental representations connected with our early experiences with significant people and the external world. In my view, for most women, family and work represent two very different 'internal objects' often experienced consciously and unconsciously as being in conflict with each other.

Is there room for both?

The aspiration to 'have it all' can also be linked to the experience of 'not being good enough'. Having 'failed' at fully engaging with both 'internal objects' – the narcissistic fantasy of having it all – one may find oneself switching to feeling not good enough.

In the following examples, I will be describing three different experiences of the 'work object' that illustrate the dynamics behind the dilemmas women face in managing the tension between work and family.

A fragile 'work object' – where is the desire?

Marion found herself either in 'menial part-time jobs' or unemployed when the children were small. She now feels she has lost her way and is working with little enjoyment and basic pay as a teaching assistant. She told me, 'I feel under stimulated and in a state of quiet despair; thinking of engaging in something more challenging seems too scary.'

Oxbridge educated and very bright, Marion opted to study law instead of science, her first love. She ended up in an administrative role that she learnt to like. After having her first child, just one week before she was due back at work, she was offered a redundancy package that she accepted.

Because of her personality and family background, she has struggled from the beginning to find her vocation. She was now looking to find a fulfilling job, but was also quite ambivalent about embarking on this search, hating the idea of spending too much time away from her children.

Behind the engagement with unwanted or unfulfilling careers is often a fragile sense of oneself and of one's own value that can lead to depression, passivity and lack of engagement with reality, as well as the feeling of not being good enough. This psychological state of mind is related to situations where the 'work object' hasn't fully developed or has been imposed from outside, often the result of parental pressure. Marion, in complying with her parents' expectations in her choice of subject at university, gradually lost the connection with her desire and ambitions for herself, despite her cleverness and potential. Raising children also became a defence against acknowledging her ambition to develop a more engaging and meaningful career.

A compulsive 'work object' – will I be able to stop?

Pamela and Lucy, both consultants in acute medicine, were accomplished professionals who had already achieved considerable success in their area of work. They knew each other, though they worked in different hospitals.

The responsibility and the complexity of their jobs were getting in the way of their raising a young family with their respective partners. They were both constantly tired and Pamela had been seriously ill on a number of occasions.

Their initial motivation for choosing their careers was linked to their family medical backgrounds and the experience of death at an early age. Pamela's mother died when she was in her teens and Lucy had the traumatic experience of seeing someone dying when she was very little.

They were very ambivalent about letting go of their original drive. At first, the thought of other career options was experienced as a threat to their primary identity, which had informed their choices from the start. A career change felt like losing their main motivation and purpose in life.

Pamela explained, 'I love my job, but it's exhausting and stressful. I'm frequently on call at the weekend, which means I can't completely switch off. I get a lot of affirmation from work, but I still think the children are my priority'; whereas Lucy told me, 'I always wanted to be a doctor. Though I remember how I resented as a teenager both my parents working very hard. I don't want my children to have the same experience of loss.'

For these two women the dilemma was particularly raw. They loved their families, but they were equally passionate about their work and their sense of vocation.

Work as a life raft

As a young art graduate, Charlotte managed to find a job in a local design company that she thoroughly enjoyed. Later on, she moved into administration and project management, needing to earn more money and wishing to work more regular hours. However, when she got married and had her first child, she found work very hard and hated leaving the baby while she went to the office. While on maternity leave for her second child, she was made redundant. At that time her husband had a permanent position and she could afford not to work.

Charlotte's own parents had gone through a difficult divorce. She was determined to provide a very different experience for her husband and children, creating a stable and supporting environment for them. That became her main focus and purpose. When the children were older, she decided to work from home, providing project-management input to a number of small companies. She didn't like the job, doing something she didn't find enriching or stimulating. However, she was keen to continue to sustain her family, which now had increasing financial demands: 'I found this very stressful, working on my own, with no one to turn to for advice. Nevertheless I managed to hold on to the work'.

Now in her fifties, at a time when her children had become independent, she wished to do something more fulfilling, although she was still reluctant to let go of her original reparative motivation: building the healthy family she never had as a child. That central drive was still very powerful and impaired her capacity to look at her work situation with fresh eyes. Her work identity was completely 'occupied' by her original need to support and enable her family.

A twin dynamic: 'work system' and 'family system'

I believe that work and family represent two separate systems for women, a *twin* dynamic. These systems require interactions, transactions and negotiations between each other; integration is often not possible. Women have to learn to move between the two systems. Metaphorically, we can liken the work system and the family system to 'twins' in the womb, who are separate and who can be in conflict for space and nourishment.

What happens if one area takes more space?

Another way of looking at the relatedness between work and family is the Gestalt concept of the figure and the ground: when we see initially one picture, with further discernment our perspective changes and we can also see a different picture.

Neither of the two systems can disappear, they are both always present, but each has more prominence at different times. We make a choice, 'we don't blend the two together' (Hirschhorn, 1999). Yet, there is often a pressure, internal and external, to engage fully with both and to ignore or underestimate the tension and conflict between the two.

Permission to choose

Although the central dilemma was the same, the outcomes for the women I've mentioned were different.

I don't know what exactly happened to Marion. At the end of our consultancy sessions she was more in touch with her ambition and her desire to find a more challenging and fulfilling career. She was considering various options, including retraining. She now seemed more capable of acknowledging she had some choices, even if these were limited.

Pamela, however, was still struggling to make a choice. Of the two medical consultants, she was the one more 'at risk' because of her poor health. She could easily become ill again, creating more stress for herself and her family. Highly intelligent and perceptive, she could clearly understand she needed to change job, but she was very hesitant to give up a career that she loved, although she was finding it very stressful. Paradoxically, her own ambivalence about her job was more of an obstacle than an additional motivation to leave. Despite the reality of practical and economic factors, she was still reluctant to give up her original reparative motivation.

Lucy, the other medical consultant, finally managed to give herself permission to resign her position and decided to stay at home for a year until her youngest child went to school. She was planning to keep some links with her organization and remain involved in a teaching role. It wasn't an easy choice: she loved her job and she was good at it. However, she could see the strain on herself and her family and she was able to give it up, though temporarily. Lucy managed to let go of her 'compulsion' to repair and resist the seduction of a narcissistic position that she could 'do it all'.

Charlotte gave herself permission to explore alternative careers and interests. However, she struggled to give up her identity as the 'family supporter' and to create the internal as well as the external space in which to explore new possibilities. Work wasn't a life raft any more: she had successfully supported and brought up her family. Her driving motivation wasn't there anymore and she felt lost without it.

The sociologist Catherine Hakin points out that: 'The vast majority of women who claim to be career-oriented discover that their priorities change after they have children' (Pinker, p. 163). She separates them into three main categories: the 'home–centred', who want to stay home full-time, the 'work–centred' whose career takes precedence, and the 'adaptive women' who try to combine children and career, drifting between various work schedules and positions, looking for 'the perfect arrangement'.

Whatever the focus or the 'arrangement', and despite the increasing number of fathers who are much more involved in childcare, this dilemma remains central to many working women's life.

This experience is very familiar: as a working mother, it has been a constant dilemma for me while I was bringing up my own children – wanting to be fully present and involved with them while trying to develop a meaningful career at the same time. I never let go of the 'work internal object'; I kept it alive, creating a *bricolage* experience, adapting and readjusting to my family's changing circumstances. My motivation was fuelled by witnessing my mother's frustrating experience: highly intelligent and very well educated, she had to let go of a potential career as a lawyer and an academic to look after her children.

Managing multiple identities is always complex, particularly when they are in competition with one another. There is a need for a third 'position', an internal management function that can facilitate the transaction between the two and make the mind fully aware of the dilemma. 'Ambivalent love' reflects the challenge of managing the two systems, *family* and *work*, and the complexity of finding balance and fulfilment in both.

Part II

Organizational consultancy in the Tavistock tradition

In this section I will be looking at what is meant by a system-psychodynamic approach and why this is relevant to leadership, management and organizational consultancy in today's changing environment, with chapters exploring: the impact of the primary task on team dynamics, consulting with individuals at the interface between a personal and professional context, the challenge of organizational succession, and leadership 'beyond textbooks'.

The chapters provide examples of complex work situations and describe how individuals, leaders and organizations have dealt with different roles and organizational challenges in the current fluid and challenging working environment.

Why a system-psychodynamic approach?

Identifying the red thread

In my experience, there is always a 'red thread' to be found beneath any client's situation: the key dynamic, issue or anxiety that lies at the core of what has been presented, though often hidden or under the surface.

The term 'system-psychodynamic' refers to the marriage between psychodynamic ideas such as unconscious feelings, transference and counter-transference, and systemic concepts such as boundaries, roles and tasks. The system-psychodynamic approach can help to identify the client's 'red thread' and provide the scaffolding and framework for understanding and addressing the dilemmas that the client – whether an individual or organization – is facing.

The challenge for the practitioner and for people in leadership and management positions is to engage with both, trying to capture the dynamics that exist under the surface in individuals and organizations, as well as paying attention to the organization as a system with its interconnections and boundaries in the context of the wider environment.

The following vignettes will illustrate some of the key concepts that lie at the core of this approach to help to connect this framework to people's experiences and dynamics in the work place, and to provide a map for those readers who are not familiar with this way of thinking.

The organization as a system

Lotus, a highly respected art organization, is fighting for survival. It has a distinguished history. The alma mater of a number of successful artists, it once provided the environment for many innovative initiatives and groundbreaking training. However, its influence has gradually faded and the organization is now struggling to find funding and sponsors.

The senior team, despite proclaiming their intention and desire to reach out, seems incapable of engaging with the larger community or of adapting their original approach to the current art world and social environment. Their 'loyalty' to the rigor and purity of their way of thinking gets in the way of them finding new connections and potential areas for intervention. Lotus represents an example of a 'closed system'.

The concept of a 'closed system' relates to the work of Miller and Rice (1967), who provided a framework for looking at organizations as *open systems* – the notion that any system can survive only by being open to the external environment. The boundary around the system needs to be both sufficiently clear and robust to separate the inside from the outside, and suitably flexible to allow an interchange with the external context.

Lotus's organizational boundary is quite rigid, allowing too little exchange with different and more commercial art institutions and the wider environment. Their focus and perspective remain mainly internal. Though the survival of art institutions has become increasingly difficult with the progressive withdrawal of public funding, Lotus's reluctance to be open to new input and receptive to the external environment is a major contributor to their difficulties. Only when a new generation of staff joins the organization does Lotus finally start to shift its focus and engage more willingly with the wider context.

Personal versus systemic

At times, it is all too easy to attribute a difficult team or organizational dynamic to specific individuals, and thereby to underestimate or ignore the *systemic* element involved in what has happened. The next example provides an illustration of this tension.

The team of a university department meets regularly to discuss their students. The discussions are lively and quite passionate about the students' performance and engagement with their course. Most of the staff know the students well. The overall tone of the conversation is usually benign; the lecturers are very involved with the students and interested in their work. However, the meeting is also an opportunity to unload their frustrations and difficulties concerning some individual situations. Katie, the department administrator, also attends. She takes the minutes and occasionally contributes to the discussion.

After a long team discussion about essays – focused on delays in submissions and concerns about the quality of the writing – Katie suddenly reveals that she regularly edited some of the essays before passing them on to the tutors. She was trying to provide some consistency in their presentation.

The team is stunned. Part of the evaluation is based on how students present their material: it is seen as data, to understand how the candidate approaches the assignment.

This example illustrates how the administrator took up a 'reparative' role connected to her conscious or unconscious perception that the tutors' approach was too critical or punitive towards the students. Though part of the same system, the administrator felt mobilized to do something different.

Even if Katie's personality played a part in what happened, this incident should be seen as a *systemic* issue. It shows how a possible lack of integration between the teaching and administrative functions, and the tension between the tasks of developing students' potential and assessing their abilities, might have caused a split within the system, creating the context for Katie to act out.

The tendency is often to treat similar incidents as mainly related to the personalities involved, rather than evidence of a systemic issue or dilemma.

The next example, concerning a whole team, is further evidence of what I mean. In this instance, the 'creative' team of a branding company was under scrutiny. Despite their exceptional creative talent, they had a reputation for being difficult and arrogant towards people in other roles. They were, of course, an essential part of the organization, often under a lot of pressure to produce ideas in a very short time.

Several of them had worked for the company for many years; they were very proud of their skills and also quite defensive of their role and position within the organization. The other teams, such as the strategy department and client services, were very different, less established and less connected to the organizational culture.

After a number of interviews, I realized that a significant part of the creative team's difficulties wasn't due to their personalities, as originally suggested by the director, but was strongly connected to a recent restructure that had cut off the creative team from the wider vision of the company. The creative team had been relegated to a 'technical role', where before they had been directly connected with the strategic team and had the opportunity to feel more involved in the whole project and design process.

Though some rigidity was clearly due to the history of their role and their personality traits, the current difficulties seemed to be very connected to *systemic issues*. The team was described as being the heart of the company, but they weren't allowed to have a say about strategic issues. I was surprised to discover that they usually didn't go to the launch of a new brand – as if they didn't want to have anything to do with the final product. The decision of relegating them to technical role had wider repercussions on the whole system and had to be reconsidered to avoid further problems.

Unconscious processes in groups

Moving on now from systems to *groups*, I would like to share a quite striking example of unconscious processes at work on a collective level. It occurred when I was at a conference, taking part in a training event to explore the relationships between different groups. The participants had to select a couple of visitors to 'visit' other groups, who were then to report back on their experience. Although the conference was held in France, the official language was English, and a number of the French participants were struggling to express themselves in English and leaning on bilingual members for help.

In the group I was facilitating there was a long debate about who to select. Time was running out fast and in the end the 'rushed' decision was to choose Pierre and Monique, two French members, neither of them fluent in English. However, the group and the selected individuals didn't appear to think that language fluency was a key criterion to consider. What was obvious to the observer (myself) was obscure to the members of the group, who were entangled in their own group dynamics and in wider systemic issues.

Perhaps inevitably, because of their poor communication skills in this context, the two representatives were quite ineffective in their roles and as a result their authority was weakened. Moreover, the choice of these two representatives reflected the group's own difficulties in dealing with the internal competition among its members and in managing feelings of rivalry and envy. Choosing the least competent members for the task represented a paradoxical avoidance of acknowledging the different levels of competence within the group.

The other dynamic at play was an ambivalence towards the staff who had organized the conference. The intergroup event became an opportunity for this group to act out their difficult feelings at being in a dependent position in relation to the staff and their unconscious wish to sabotage the event the staff had set up.

This vignette shows how groups can be affected by powerful dynamics that are often unconscious. The psychoanalyst Wilfred Bion and other authors have described how the work task is often 'disturbed' by a number of anti-task dynamics that, if not understood and addressed, can strongly affect the effectiveness of a group.

Bion (1961) developed a framework to identify some of the key unconscious dynamics in groups. He differentiated between 'work-group mentality' and 'basic assumption mentality', when the group tries to avoid engaging with the task.

In this example, the learning task at the conference gave an opportunity to members and staff to reflect on and review what had happened and try to understand why. However, in everyday work settings, it can be quite challenging to spot the dynamics and identify the motivations that mobilize individuals and groups to take certain positions or act in ways that go against the task and objectives of the organization.

Organization in the mind

People's difficulties in developing effective teamwork and constructive collaboration across different systems are also connected to holding different and even divergent 'mental representations' of their organization – linked to the concept *organization in the mind* – as described in the following example (Armstrong, 2005).

Paul is the lively leader of Green, a unit of Marsh – a well-known charity in the field mental of health. His area of work is particularly challenging as he has to liaise with government agencies, pressure groups and very complex and demanding clients. He is both highly regarded and criticized for his approach and radical views.

Though he is very demanding of himself, he is quite laidback with his leadership team, which often acts without consulting him. The unit led by Paul is regularly placed under scrutiny because of its radical views on mental health issues and its innovative practices. Paul's relaxed approach is frequently under fire from senior management and the board, while his team, thought to be quite supportive, lacks a coherent and shared approach.

I started to realize that the different constituencies of Marsh had quite contrasting *organizations in the mind*. It became clear that some of the conflicts between subsystems and the lack of internal consistency and shared views were related to divergent 'internal' models of the organization.

This emerged very vividly during a consultancy session when I asked representatives of the whole organization to make a drawing of their mental picture of Marsh. Many of the images seemed strikingly different and unconnected, as if they were describing different organizations.

'Organization in the mind' or the 'work place within' – as described by Hirschhorn (1988) – refers to the idea that each member holds a distinctive internal representation of their organization. These internal images are often different from those of other members and can even be conflicting. Though partly unconscious, they can have a powerful impact on the experience and behaviour of members of the organization, leading to misunderstandings, polarizations and potential conflicts.

Containment

I mentioned already previously the concept of organizational containment – the idea that organizations should provide a safe environment where people could feel held and 'contained'. The consequences of a lack of organizational containment can have a destructive effect on the individual, as the following example demonstrates.

On the first day that Mary arrived at her new school, nobody was there to greet her. The headmistress was away and no one seemed to know that the new head of science was starting that day. After wandering around the school on her own, she decided to go back home.

Despite being an experienced teacher, she found herself feeling quite diso-rientated: the school was unfamiliar, as well as the community it served, where she had just relocated. Her initial experience stayed with her for a long time and affected her sense of belonging and trust in the school.

She later realized that what had happened to her wasn't unusual. Though the school's approach to children, families and staff was friendly and relaxed, there was often a sense of unclear boundaries and structures and a loose framework to support staff. Mary felt that the lack of 'containment' from the organization had a negative affect both on the internal relationships and the learning task.

Bion talks of *containment* as being the capacity of the mother to respond to her baby's distress and to tolerate and transform his/her bad feelings (Bion, 1963). To be able to work effectively, people need to be part of 'containing structures' that provide enough sense of 'holding' and context to develop their capacity to be productive and creative.

A containing leading figure and well-thought-out organizational structures help people to engage with complex and demanding tasks, and to manage the anxiety related to their responsibilities and roles. If organizational and man-agement containments are weak or unclear, this usually has a negative impact on people's performance and wellbeing.

Anxiety

Lack of organizational containment can provoke *anxiety*, despite people's competence and motivation. Anxiety can also originate from unrealistic organizational expectations or a lack of alignment between our sense of self and competence and the role we are in, as shown in the next example.

Josh is a consultant who specializes in diabetic treatments. He is passionate about his field and quite well known for his research and practice in this area.

Though highly motivated in his clinical work, he finds the management side of his job extremely challenging. He exhibits high levels of anxiety both in managing his team and when engaging with the leadership of the hospital. The contrast between his ability and confidence as a clinician and his uncer-tainty and anxiety as a manager is striking. It is as if there are two different Joshes.

His appearance is often quite scruffy and unkempt, almost in an attempt to hide his seniority and role. When he was young he excelled at school, but struggled to be accepted by his peers and was also the subject of unpleasant bullying. His father, never particularly supportive when he was growing up, remains critical and quite dismissive towards him.

In our work together, Josh begins to understand that the source of his *anxiety* around managing and leading stems from his lack of internal authority, originating in his early experience within his family and at school. Taking up a more visible authority position within his hospital becomes almost unbear-able. While he can own his authority and expertise in his clinical work, he can't see himself as a credible leader – it's as if his father's critical voice is always whispering in his ears.

Anxiety is a symptom of the fear of losing control of our rational self and of the risk of more primitive and irrational emotions taking over. Anxiety, a concept as defined by Freud, Klein, Meltzer and others, is often evidence of complex early experiences and relationships we haven't been able to work through. As Josh's story shows, anxieties can profoundly affect our lives and work situations unless we can identify and address the underlying issues.

Anxiety can also come from the organizational task, as the following vignette demonstrates.

Mark, a senior manager in a global energy company, Gasten, is finding his job increasingly challenging. His team of young and talented engineers seem to be struggling to carry on with their tasks and some of them want to leave the organization.

They are building a new infrastructure in Africa, employing mainly local people. Though they recognize the importance of involving the local community, there are strong concerns about their level of competence and their safety standards. The international press has also expressed great reservations about the impact of this huge infrastructure on the environment. Gasten has invested a substantial amount of money in community and 'green' projects; however, the wider concerns haven't gone away.

This new generation of engineers, in their twenties and thirties, have found it difficult to justify their involvement in this project to themselves, their friends and families at home and to the local community. They have felt tarnished by the overall task, despite its interesting technical challenges.

There have also been reports of a number of technical mistakes that could have been prevented. Mark wonders if the lack of alignment with the organizational objective is partly behind what is happening: their anxiety and ambivalence towards their task make the engineers less focused and more vulnerable.

The primary task, or tasks, of an organization inevitably create some related anxiety. There is always a *shadow anxiety* behind challenging and stressful tasks. For example, working in a hospital environment can evoke powerful anxiety about death, while a job in the financial sector can raise anxiety about bankruptcy and financial collapse. To minimize these anxieties, organizations often develop a number of defences that, at times, can limit people's ability to perform a meaningful task. In her seminal study on 'Social system against anxiety', Isabel Menzies describes how institutional defences against difficult and painful nursing tasks diminished nurses' motivation and sense of purpose (Menzies, 1988).

Understanding the *shadow primary anxiety* behind the organizational task can help to address people's stress in their work situation and to develop more appropriate institutional defences without impairing people's job satisfaction and belief in their contribution.

In the following chapters I will be using some of the concepts illustrated above to discuss my work with clients and my hypotheses about their individual and organizational dynamics. I will also be referring to other concepts and ideas such as the *attachment theory* (Bowlby), *valency* (Bion) and the *unthought known* (Bollas). In the next chapter, I describe how the nature of the task affects the behaviour and mental health of a team – what I called the *sponge affect*. All of these concepts can help us to identify the 'red thread' that lies hidden at the core of the issues that affect our working lives, both as individuals and as members of teams.

1   The team as a sponge★

How the nature of the task affects the
behaviour and mental life of a team

In my capacity as organizational consultant to a number of teams in the caring
professions, I am constantly struck by the fact that similar individuals or
groups can behave in extremely diverse ways when working with different
client groups.

In this chapter, I will be discussing my experiences with four teams
working respectively with chronically mentally ill patients, young people who
take drugs, abused children and adolescents. Their contexts, organizational
frameworks and structures are different, but in each case the flavour of what
it is like to work with their client groups lies right at the heart of the consultancy relationship. There is no hiding from the dynamics of each team's
experience, if one is prepared to see it. The core issues of their tasks and the
challenges they face are laid bare in front of the consultant.

'The team as a sponge' is a crucial, fascinating but dangerous area of work
and research for the consultant. The term 'sponge' describes the striking way
in which a team absorbs and soaks up the central dynamics which operate
within its client group, often without realizing that this is happening. This
process can also be described as 'mirroring' or 'reflection process', as in casework supervision, when the relationship between client and worker is
reflected in the relationship between worker and supervisor (Mattinson,
1992).

> The core idea is that dynamic interactions that belong and originate in
> the area of relationship are acted out in an adjacent area as though they
> belong there, being carried from one area to the other by a 'player'
> common to both.
>
> (Hughes and Pengelly, 1997, p. 83)

This chapter explores the complexities of dealing with the core issues of an
organization in a group setting, and of unfolding the team's dilemmas and
difficulties in a way that can be worked on. Understanding the 'sponge effect'
can be translated into meaningful actions and changes within the team, and
can help the staff to reach a more mature approach to its task. But the consultant has to be prepared to be a sponge herself, to soak up the group's

projections, in order to help the staff to identify the main processes affecting them.

Fundamental to this approach is being open to the experience and to the projections of the people to whom you are consulting. This often implies experiencing very uncomfortable feelings.

Only through a constant review of the consultant's own feelings and emotions, and holding on to the uncertainty of the experience, resisting the pressure to give immediate answers and advice to the client organization, and bearing the anxiety of 'getting nowhere', it is possible to reach some understanding of the underlying dynamics which affect the whole organizational process and uncover the core issues with which they are struggling (see Chapter 2).

When I cross the boundary of an organization that I am consulting to, I am usually full of my own concerns and thoughts, which are often completely unrelated to the life of that particular organization or group. I sometimes feel quite unprepared and reluctant to be open to the team's projections, to listen to and tune into what is going on. I know it is going to be difficult, harder than I would like it to be. And then I am suddenly 'hit' by the mood of the group, by their undercurrent. The four examples which follow illustrate what I mean.

Resistance in Cherry House

Team A sit with their backs to the wall, waiting for my interventions. They say very little and look at me in a sleepy, absent way, while I struggle to get their attention and to encourage them to reflect on their work and their difficulties.

Team A works in a hostel for chronically mentally ill people. Most of its residents have come directly from the street. Cherry House is often these clients' first permanent home after years of neglect and wandering in and out of psychiatric hospitals. Team A is a 'nice' team: people are kind to each other, to me and to their manager. Their 'niceness' has a quality of lifelessness, however. People seem unable to present issues and thoughts about their work. I feel the pressure of having to cajole them into engaging with me. I find myself constantly asking questions about their practice and trying to make the situation livelier.

The only time the team comes alive is when accidents or crises have occurred. It is as if this gives them an immediate task to deal with rather than having to wait for the inexorable passing of time. Hospitalization of residents is both hoped for and dreaded by the staff. It brings failure as well as respite: failure for having been unable to keep the residents in the community; respite from the boredom and repetitiveness of their tasks and from the exposure to profound disturbance.

A new regime has created a different ethos from the previous one: emphasis is now on rehabilitating patients, making them more responsible for their lives, encouraging initiatives and collaboration on house tasks, with a view to moving most of the residents on to semi-independent accommodation. Dependency is discouraged and a considerable autonomy is seen as the ultimate goal of the team's interventions. Rationally, the staff have accepted and embraced the new approach: they have engaged in the plans and expressed cooperation and interest in the new developments. But in reality they find it incredibly difficult to implement any real change. For example, the plan for residents to organize their meals and participate in the cooking falls by the wayside. Most of the time, the staff are the ones who do all the work. The dependent relationship at the core of their work does not seem to alter.

Amy, the deputy manager, wants to talk about rehabilitation. She thinks the staff are not clear about this concept. People do not respond to her request: they want to talk about Karl, a resident who keeps causing problems. 'Karl was almost going to blow up at lunch', a care worker says. Others do not seem worried: 'He's all right now'. Someone else complains about the handover which is not working; relevant information is exchanged informally.

Amy suggests that there were signs of Karl's distress. He talked to himself a lot, put on funny voices and wet himself. Nobody seemed to notice.

I comment on their wish to keep the situation quiet, to reassure themselves that, on the whole, everything is fine. Having to acknowledge that what happened is not all right would force them to face a number of dilemmas. They have to think about creating a tighter structure around Karl and considering the possibility of discharging him, which they feel quite guilty about.

I pick up an enormous reluctance to make any plan or commitment to change anything: the handover, the way the meals are organized, etc. It is as if engaging more with the structures and with the running of the hostel they will lose their 'immunity' to the awfulness of working with such a difficult and disturbing client group.

My experience of the team's passivity and their inability to engage in a dialogue with me mirrors their experience with their static and dependent residents. The staff, too, keeps trying to enliven and motivate the residents and to make their lives fuller through rehabilitation plans, activities and ideas for discharge. Like their residents, they use a passive resistance to my various attempts to review their working practice and to reflect on how the work might be done differently.

Staff talk about the residents as if they were little children who need constant help, guidance and supervision (if only you could forget their age, their disturbance and their odd behaviour!). It is difficult for them to acknowledge to me and to each other the unpleasantness of working with people who have dropped out of society, who cannot develop proper relationships, and who show so little will to change or improve. Despite the apparent shift towards active rehabilitation, the staff continue to put most of their effort into maintaining positive relationships with the residents and also with me. This serves to shield them from the full power of the negative and from the fear of a violent eruption, which can jeopardize years of work and put the staff's reputation, as well as their achievements, at risk. The emphasis in Cherry House is on maintaining a good dependent relationship, which provides invisible armour for the staff against the ambivalent feelings about their task.

Winnicott, in his seminal paper 'Hate in the Counter Transference' (1947/1958), describes the importance of acknowledging the feelings of hate in the relationship between mother and baby and between therapist and patient. Only when the hate is recognized can the treatment really progress and have an impact. Cherry House staff cannot let their hatred emerge. But denying their negative feelings makes them unable to engage in a more dynamic therapeutic relationship. The team is trapped between two contrasting models of care that Miller and Gwynne (1972) have vividly described as a 'warehouse' and a 'horticultural' model. Both models can be used to repress hate.

Abandoned Orchard Lodge

Team B is mute. The temporary manager who has represented the team's first experience of good management for a long time is leaving. The group's usually lively meeting is now dead. There are no words to express their feelings of abandonment and worthlessness. There is only emptiness. I seem to be talking to myself.

Orchard Lodge is a therapeutic community for abused children. The unit has a troubled history. It was created 12 years ago with an ambitious brief: to care for and treat young children who have been traumatized in early life by long-term physical and emotional abuse. Its founders 'abandoned' the project early on and left it under the umbrella of Bencar, an organization with little experience in this field. Orchard Lodge had to struggle for many years to survive in a context of many management changes and constant financial difficulties.

Like children from a 'dysfunctional family', the staff often feel abandoned and unworthy of proper attention, leadership and care.

At the root of their difficulties in creating and maintaining a healthy organization is the unbearable element at the heart of their task: having to deal with the breaking of the ultimate taboo between adults and children, namely child abuse. Often, when faced with an internal crisis the team react as if they are incapable of exercising control or authority, or as if they are unworthy proper leadership and guidance.

The session starts with Felix, a team leader, explaining how difficult it has been during the weekend. The children were restless and it was difficult to contain them. The previous week a manager from headquarters had a meeting at Orchard Lodge to explain the financial difficulties the organization is facing and the need to make savings on all fronts. People report this back in a remarkably calm and thoughtful way. Then there is a short silence and I ask them what they are thinking.

Wendy says she feels guilty: she forgot to take the children to therapy twice last week. Other care workers comment that Stephen, the psycho-therapist, should remind them and there should be a different system. In Orchard Lodge there are 'the thinkers and the doers' someone says. I suggest that in this case the doers are the care staff who assume the parental role, and who feel ambivalent about therapy. They often have to convince or drag the children to therapy, maybe having to interrupt something they enjoy doing together. On the other hand, people did not dare to ask the therapist to change some sessions during half-term, which conflicted with an interesting outing, as if there were no possibility of negotiating a different time. The perception and the ambivalence about authority are, in this case, located in the relationship with the therapist, in his role as a senior staff member. The therapist is sabotaged, left waiting and forgotten, while, at the same time, he is experienced as rigid and inflexible. The discussion leads to some awareness of this relationship and the implications for other relations with authority figures within the system; awareness of their constant struggle between sabo-tage and fear of negotiation.

As Walker points out, 'Adult abuse survivors easily get caught into a generalized feeling that everything is beyond their control, as it was in their childhood, whereas in adulthood some things are not.' (Walker, 1997, p. 101). In a similar fashion, Orchard Lodge staff often behave as if they did not have any choice or say in what was happening to the unit. In situations of stress the staff behaviour seems to move between a 'blaming' model – like an abuser 'in search of a victim', and a hopeless and paralysed model – being the victim, with no sense of worth or of potential effectiveness.

Hughes and Pengelly (1997) use the Karpman (1968) drama triangle, com-prising the roles of persecutor, rescuer and victim, to illustrate the shift of roles between care worker and client and between supervisor and supervisee. In Orchard Lodge this triangular dynamic is emphasized by the nature of the task. Different members of staff and management move constantly between these three positions. I also shift between these three roles, both in terms of my own experience and in the way I am perceived by Orchard Lodge's staff. I find it difficult to stay with these three dimensions and to accept that they are part of my own experience of my role and function, as well as their experience of me.

As I feel deeply committed to the staff's development and growth, it is hard not to feel a victim when staff describe my sessions as not being effective or if they claim that our work together does not help their practice on the floor. At the same time, it is also easy to be carried away when there are signs of progress in their work and good results with the children. It is hard to resist feeling that my input was the essential ingredient for their development and success.

The aggressive or 'perpetrator' feelings are often a reaction to some of their failings, or to the repetitiveness of their dynamics. I then experience a deep wish to dump them, or I fantasize that they should close down and end their abortive attempts to make the project work. All these feelings and fantasies are deeply connected with the pain and struggle of their task, and with the constant adjustments that have to be made between the possible and the impossible, in relation to the children and to themselves.

The chief motivation for staff to work with this client group is their wish to make an impact, to promote meaningful shifts, and to repair some of the damages inflicted on the lives of the children in their care. Some damage is beyond repair, but some can be healed. It is the notion that things are still possible that generates hope and creates opportunities for a deeper understanding that can result in some real changes. Sometimes my task is to help the team to move from the area of the possible to the area of the impossible, in order to help them realize that some children in their care cannot be healed, that some irreparable damage has taken place – and that both children and staff must learn to live with it.

Hostility in Harbour Centre

Team C eye each other with hostility. Once again, someone is under the spotlight for having done something wrong. People look uncomfortable and angry. There is an atmosphere of blame and a sense of contempt for the hypotheses I put forward.

Harbour Centre provides initial support and information for drug users. It is a relatively new unit, which has brought together staff who are used to working autonomously in the community. The team has been 'motherless and homeless' for some time. The original manager left, and for a couple of years there were internal staff difficulties and there was no acting figure of authority either outside or within the system. Rose has recently been appointed as the new team manager. She is experienced in the field and interested in developing the new post, but finds it difficult to assert her authority over the team. After a brief honeymoon the team has started to sabotage her initiatives and does not engage with her proposals.

Harbour Centre's core task is to try to introduce users to a network of services, which provide treatment and detoxification programmes.

The staff come from a 'community culture' where individual staff have learnt to rely mainly on their own skills in dealing with very disturbing and complex situations, without the protection of a clearly identifiable organization or of a respected professional status.

Being able to work on your own means that you don't have to rely very much on others. It can create the illusion that you do not need others. Like their clients, the staff of Harbour Centre often function in 'survival mode', a sort of street ethos where you can only feel safe if you rely on yourself, since nobody else can really be trusted. This is connected with an anti-authoritarian stance, a strong sense of advocacy in relation to the drug users who are seen as the victims of very difficult circumstances – a sense of wanting to repair some of the damage inflicted on them by family and society. And finally, working independently creates a sense of freedom, of fewer organizational ties and less control from the overall system.

When working with drug addiction, the staff constantly face issues of trust, dependency and disruptive behaviour. These issues have been very much at the core of the consultancy process. It has been almost impossible to create an atmosphere of trust in which staff can examine the way they function as a team and accept help in understanding and working through some of their difficulties. Their negative feelings towards each other, their self-centred perspective and their contempt for my contribution parallel their own experience of working with clients who do not value others, and who do not have any sense of worth in themselves.

Rose, Harbour Centre's team manager, starts the session by expressing her anxiety about Charles, a staff member who, while working with some clients in a council estate, was involved in a confrontation between drug dealers and the police. He was hurt, but not seriously. People ask for details about what happened. Rose knows very little. We discover that she has not managed to ask Charles to report back to her. The need for debriefing in order to understand what happened has been overlooked. Rose's authority and responsibility have not been recognized by the staff or by herself. I point out the need to reclaim responsibility and accountability within the team, together with the need to give Charles support and guidance.

Behind Rose's inability to negotiate with Charles is also her anger with a worker who absconds and behaves in an anarchic and unorthodox way. It is the same worker who sits, session after session, always with his coat and hat on, regarding my efforts to consult to the team with scorn and contempt. He is the one who often ends the sessions for me and who laughs and giggles with his pal or adopts quite threatening behaviour. At the end of this session Rose and the other staff are more aware of the part they play in avoiding control, and of the risks of relinquishing their authority and responsibility.

Although the staff are often at the receiving end of abusive and aggressive behaviour, feelings of hatred towards their clients never come up in the sessions. The staff's hatred is often displaced in their relationships with each other, with management and with myself. I often feel unheard, unappreciated and not worthy of their trust, which I relate to their experience with the drug users, in a context where there is no sense of a benign authority or of positive dependency.

We see here a situation of fear of dependency in an environment where dependency is associated with something bad (i.e. drugs), which makes you unable to lead an independent and full life.

> There is a vast difference between those patients who have had satisfactory early experiences which can be discovered in the transference and those whose very early experiences have been so deficient and distorted

that the analyst has to be the first in the patient's life to supply certain environmental essentials.

(Winnicott, 1947, p. 198)

What Winnicott describes has strong similarities with my work with Harbour Centre's team. Their primary experience has been of 'organizational deprivation' where there has been no 'good experience' of management or organizational life.

Reflecting on, and looking critically and constructively at their practice is a virtually impossible task. Occasionally people do make a small shift: the blame on one member of staff is defused, someone shares some difficult feelings about a client, and the manager plans a Friday meeting for the handover of the most difficult cases. However, the team's fundamental inability to think does not change and I struggle to maintain my clarity of thought.

The pervasive effect of their attacks on the setting and on myself stay with me during the week, and I often dread going back. It is the hopelessness and the self-disruptiveness of the drug addiction that contaminate any attempt to develop a relationship. My attempt to provide the 'environmental essentials' does not get very far. I can only survive their attacks and feed back to them what I think is going on.

My attempts to help the Harbour Centre team to see the 'sponge effect' in the dynamic of their relationships were not successful. Maybe that also mirrored their working situation, where the success rate is very low.

Arguments in Ivy Street

Team D is arguing about who has the vision of the organization and who is entitled to decide their approach and working methods. The positions are rigid and dogmatic: everyone knows best, there is no space for differences.

Ivy Street is a day centre which provides counselling for adolescents. The manager, Ruth, has been in her post for many years and has developed a distinctive approach to intervention with adolescents. This specific approach is not officially acknowledged: staff are implicitly expected to work in a particular way without any clear recognition of what it is. Nevertheless, Ruth and her deputy have great faith in this approach, which they regard as unique and the best available. They think it provides containment and support through its setting of tight boundaries and well-thought-out principles. The manager is the main source of supervision and expertise within the centre. The use of different methods or external interventions is not only discouraged, but almost forbidden. Differences of opinion are not taken on board because their method is seen as the only effective way of engaging young people in treatment and counselling. Inevitably, staff are resentful about not having a voice and not being able to influence the development of their practice.

The development of a centralized approach seemed necessary because many of the staff were either part-time or very inexperienced, and also because Ivy Street workers were spread throughout a large geographical area. However, the centralization of expertise in one person has created a dependency culture, with very little sense that staff can grow or develop. Internal negotiations are very difficult: there is tension and conflict between the manager and the staff. Each side is unable to see the other's point of view. This dynamic mirrors perfectly the ambivalence of parents who cannot trust adolescents to find their own way, and the core dilemma for parents of how to balance necessary limit-setting and guidance, with space for individual discovery. There is an atmosphere in Ivy Street of a closed system, with no nourishment coming from outside.

From the beginning I felt that I was walking in a minefield, and that I had to guard myself from the traps of a 'family dispute'. I had to be very careful to keep my distance and my boundary position. At the same time, I felt the pain that this family dispute was creating among staff members, particularly in the 'parental' pair, Lucy and her deputy.

I have been constantly struck by the fundamentalist tone of the debate within the Ivy Street team and by the deep antagonism between the 'faithful' and the 'unfaithful'. The 'faithful' being the ones who consider their approach unique and irreplaceable (mainly the manager and her deputy). The 'unfaithful' those who want change, different input and even a new leadership.

This unique culture reflects one of the central dynamics of adolescence: the need for dogma and absolute certainty in a context of profound psychological and physical changes. The impulses of adolescence and emergent sexuality are rigidly controlled by a dogmatic culture. Adolescents' uncertainty about life and the future, their conflicting needs, are channelled into a rigid container. Differences are too complex to be tolerated. Diversity of opinion is experienced and treated as 'delinquency' or rebellion by the staff and management. There is a sense of claustrophobia when there does not seem to be enough space for different views. I feel both compelled to take sides and to observe in a neutral capacity, as if making connections and being able to see different points of view is a very dangerous business. Dogmatism and rigidity become defences which seem to make the uncertainties and responsibilities of moving into adulthood more bearable.

The way the manager and her deputy perceive criticism and requests for change from the staff, and the way the need for change is put forward by the staff, have the dramatic tones of a Greek tragedy, of an impending catastrophe, as if only by 'killing the parents' will the young person develop a separate identity. In discussing Bion's ideas on 'catastrophic change' (Bion, 1970), Copley describes:

> how change that is necessary for change can be dreaded and disruptive to the group ... the idea necessary for change needs to be made available for use without implementation of the accompanying sense of catastrophe arising from the dynamic disruptive impact of the new alongside the old.
>
> (Copley, 1993, pp. 27, 28)

There is little room for a negotiation space where parents and children – managers and staff – can collaborate. My task as a consultant is to enable the team to separate the ideas for change from the associated idea of catastrophe: that is, to be the guardian of a potential space (Winnicott, 1971) where some negotiation and mutual understanding can take place.

How managers can run healthier and more effective organizations

The organizations I have been describing are very different, as are my relationships with them. Their circumstances vary enormously as regards their structures and resources, the therapeutic potential of their interventions and the quantity and quality of disturbance of their client groups. An understanding of the sponge effect, of the projections coming from the client group, can only work and be effective in a context where the majority of people involved have a sense of structure, roles and accountability. This is not easy in a world where organizations are no longer able any more to provide enough containment for negative projections and do not provide a dependable environment (Miller, 1993; Stokes, 2019).

It is the managers who increasingly have to provide that containment and support, while being able to tolerate negative projections from staff as well as clients. Yet the managers of Cherry House, Orchard Lodge, Harbour Centre and Ivy Street have a great deal of responsibility and not much authority to go with it. In other words, they are answerable for their units, but do not have the right to make the ultimate decision or to make decisions which are binding on others (Obholzer, 2019).

They have to juggle scarce resources, regulate pressures and requests from the client group and respond to demands from staff in order to provide better support and provision for them. The manager's role requires being inside the system, having an in-depth understanding of the clients' and staff's needs, and being sufficiently outside of it to get an overall view of the organization in its environment. In other words, the manager has to hold what Miller has described as a 'boundary position'. It is a difficult role to perform competently. It requires both paternal and maternal skills, an ability to move constantly between inside and outside the system, great resilience to pressure and demand, self-containment and some capacity to stand alone.

Consultancy can enhance these skills and can be an essential key to understanding what is required for holding this inside/outside position. It requires the ability to bear people's negative feelings in order to help staff stay in touch with the essence of their job. In a similar way, managers should be able to develop an ability to tolerate their staff's projections while maintaining a boundary position.

To facilitate this process, my consultancy to teams in the helping professions always includes separate sessions with the team manager. The individual session provides the manager with an opportunity to look at team's issues in a more systemic way, to look more directly at his or her role and function, and to address problems that might not be possible to raise in the group session. The intention of this session is to support and model the manager's inside/outside position and to offer a specific place for looking at the sponge effect within the organization as a whole.

★★★

The new manager of Orchard Lodge, the therapeutic community for abused children, is now in place. He has to face a number of problems. For instance, three staff members have handed in their resignation yet seem very reluctant to engage in a formal leaving process. All three are off sick and do not seem able to return.

The team is furious with them but seem powerless and unable to take any action. We explore in the group sessions what has happened and the possible reasons behind the three staff members' difficulties in saying goodbye properly.

The same theme is explored with the manager, who appears very eager to negotiate with the three staff, but finds it difficult to adopt a firmer position towards them. I realize how strong my wish is to force the 'absconders' to come back. I fantasize about retaliating against them, while the manager seems to be much more in touch with understanding and forgiving feelings. The children have been calmer since his arrival. There has not been any serious acting out or disruptive behaviour.

The staff express anger and resistance to yet another change of management through absconding and being disruptive. In the individual sessions, we look at the manager's own difficulties in taking a firmer stance, at his need to be perceived as a good and caring manager. He begins to see how difficult it is for anyone to openly assume a more clearly authoritative role for fear of being perceived as a potentially negative figure or 'perpetrator'. I manage to see from my own feelings how strong is the wish to punish, to retaliate, which is the dynamic the manager tries to keep at bay with his soft approach.

Eventually all the three staff members come back, however briefly, to say goodbye to staff and children.

The session with the manager is a 'role consultancy', firmly linked to the organization in which both the role and the organization are in focus. Staff who are struggling to recognize differences and diversities between themselves do not find it easy to accept this model of intervention. There is often a fear of an unhealthy and collusive alliance between consultant and manager. In reality, the model strengthens the alliance between the consultant and manager in relation to the organization's task and can provide a better holding of the consultancy process. This model should help the managers to make use of what Keats has described as 'negative capability', a particular ability to 'be' in the middle of uncertainty without pressing for certainties, facts and answers (Keats, 1817; Lanzara, 1993).

★★★

The approach to consultancy that I have described in this chapter is based on the concept that the experience projected onto the consultant is a fundamental tool that can be used to understand some of the central issues which affect the life of an organization: the capacity to listen to one's own experience, to hear the message coming from the client is central to my consultancy work. This is also true for staff and managers of organizations: if they are able to identify some of the projections coming from clients, they are much more likely to be in touch with the core issues of the task they are trying to perform.

These organizations work with client groups that society tends to forget and to exclude, or who are mainly remembered when a major crisis or violent episode occurs. In simplistic terms it could be said that society wants to lock away the mad, punish the abusers, clean up the drug addicts, be tough with difficult adolescents. The organizations I have described have to soak up the powerful dynamic of their clients' systems: the passivity and disengagement of the chronically mentally ill; the sense of worthlessness and betrayal of abused children; the desperate anger and self-destructiveness of drug addicts; the arrogance and dogmatism of adolescents. In addition, these organizations have to deal with the projections and expectations that society puts into them: they are expected to contain, to treat and to detoxify, to support. In essence, they are expected to protect and purify society from the negative and disruptive dynamics that these client groups inevitably bring with them.

When teams and managers are able to identify some of these dynamics and disentangle themselves from the web and the power of their effects, they can leave their 'psychic prisons' (Morgan, 1986); they can free up some energy to engage with the task in a more effective and creative way. They can also recognize that understanding what is happening to them is the key to the treatment of their client groups.

Note

* 'The team as a sponge' is an updated version of a paper first published in R. French and R. Vince, *Group Relations Management and Organizations*, Oxford University Press, 1999.

2 Vulnerable leadership

Consultancy to management in transition

As a relatively young consultant, I was suddenly confronted with a complex and challenging situation in my consultancy work for Sage House, a residential establishment for adolescents that was part of the Rainbow foundation, which deals with children in need. The personal elements in this project were particularly powerful and painful, obscuring at times the organizational elements at play. It was a seminal experience and offered me a steep learning curve.

A number of colleagues helped me behind the scenes to deal with my emotional response and to engage with the multiple dimensions of the project. This showed me the importance of having a third perspective, to articulate my understanding and initial hypotheses with someone else and to share my concerns and anxiety with colleagues who were one step removed.

This chapter focuses on a specific phase of this consultancy project, when I felt greatly drawn into the organization because of a major tragedy involving its director. It illustrates some of the dilemmas and challenges of the consultant's role and provides some ideas on how these can be addressed 'in practice'.

Boundaries are a constant preoccupation in our professional work and issues of boundaries were a central theme in this particular consultancy. In this instance, the boundaries were related to my role in trying to draw a division between organizational problems and personal problems, and between individual issues and group issues, while simultaneously keeping lines of communication open between everyone involved.

When a personal tragedy strikes, any negotiated boundaries seem to collapse or to blur and the usual parameters may not apply. These sorts of situations also pose important questions for a consultant about what the boundaries are when something of a personal nature profoundly affects the life of an organization. How does he or she renegotiate his or her role and function in this context?

The beginning

Sage House was facing major changes with the unexpected illness of its director and, a few months later, the arrival of a new acting head. The unit had a troubled past. Having been closed for a number of years because of internal difficulties and conflicts, it had been reopened five years previously by Rob, a new director. He had managed to draw together a team of professionals who were eager and committed to investing in the project; but despite their efforts and initial enthusiasm, the reopening had not been easy. The small client group had mirrored the uncertainty of that fresh start with a lot of acting out. They challenged the newly appointed staff, honing in on their weakness and shortcomings, and provoking incidents. The uncertainty and instability of the situation was expressed through a high level of absenteeism among the residential social workers, and a rather ambivalent commitment from the senior staff.

There had been a number of conflicts among the senior staff, which made it very difficult for them to act and intervene within the unit in a coherent and collaborative way. These conflicts were mainly around issues of authority and territory; they were an expression of the group's uncertainty and anxiety about the viability of the project. They wondered individually and collectively, consciously and unconsciously, if they would be strong enough to deal with the many disruptive projections the client group was constantly throwing at them. The pain and struggle of the young people in their care, within a framework that was still fragile and relatively new, posed a significant challenge. They were resisting rather than being able to think ahead.

The director, who had been very much at the heart of the reopening of Sage House, was also dealing with his own ambivalence. He was involved in many other commitments outside the unit, which made it impossible for him to be fully engaged inside the organization.

Order and chaos

After this difficult beginning, the unit gradually started to settle down, particularly with the arrival of a new deputy, Jane, whose presence, style and consistency helped the team to be more hopeful about the future without feeling constantly haunted by their troubled past. Her arrival marked the beginning of a new stage.

The unit felt symbolically better held and, although their thinking and planning were still focused on the short-term and the levels of authority within the staff group were not clearly defined, their work with the young people was progressing.

During this period I was working with the senior staff, while also acting as a consultant to the director and his deputy in a separate setting, in order to build on their dual role and to strengthen this level of Sage House's management structure.

Memories of bitter and disruptive conflicts in the past, combined with a desire to preserve hope and positive feelings in the role of the director, made it difficult for healthy confrontation and challenge between members of the team. My role became one of confronting them on the issues they were finding difficult to acknowledge openly, such as Rob and Jane's difficulty in meeting together and starting to negotiate their different roles and areas of responsibility within Sage House. At some level, senior staff seemed to share an implicit agreement not to confront Rob openly about the way he was directing the unit or about his ambivalence about taking full responsibility and charge of the House.

During this period Rob was not very well and was away from the unit quite often, provoking some resentment amongst the staff about his being present but not really present there. The staff felt the burden of having to carry on working without adequate support and guidance. The psychologist, Daniel, who had shared the original vision for the unit with Rob, finally took the step of hiring a locum for him, forcing Rob to make a decision about his health.

The following day the director went to hospital, where he was in and out for a number of months.

Illness and loss

The senior staff were facing a number of *dilemmas*:

* What was it possible for them to achieve in the absence of their leader?
* Were they just 'holding the fort' or could they develop the organization themselves, which was still relatively new?
* How did they reconcile their conflicting feelings of anger and resentment with sadness and compassion for their director?
* How could they provide a sense of direction for the rest of the staff and for their clients, without denying the absence of the director and the transitional nature of that period?

While Rob was away, the senior staff worked well together, despite the organizational context still being quite unsettled. Rob's absence had liberated new energy in them; his absence had also given greater space to the deputy to be more effective.

The staff were very conflicted about Rob's absence as they felt guilty about using his absence as a way of developing their own roles and authority, but they were also feeling disappointed with him for letting them down. At a different level they were mirroring the intrinsic guilt, the unconscious phantasy of adolescence that growing up means taking the parents' place, which is an aggressive act, a 'murder' (Winnicott, 1969).

The survivor's main feeling in a disaster is guilt, but 'the survivor suffers less … if he has been brave and self-sacrificing, has taken risks to help others or is injured' (Menzies, 1989, p. 250). In a similar fashion the staff were incredibly committed to making the unit work.

After a few months, the senior staff started to talk about Rob's return as he seemed better and had reacted well to his treatment. We worked together on his re-entry, on other people's ambivalence, and the effect of his absence and imminent return on the rest of the staff and on the young people.

I suggested that Rob might want to discuss his re-entry to the unit with me. It was with this agenda that I met him a couple of weeks later, completely unaware that the situation was now very different.

When Rob came to see me I was expecting to talk about his hopes and plans for Sage House, and about his mixed feelings with respect to reengaging with the organization. When he told me that he was terminally ill and had not much longer to live, I felt overwhelmed and deeply shocked. However, despite my sadness and confusion, I immediately knew that my task was to help the organization to carry on; I had to manage my sorrow and my compassion for Rob in order to maintain a sense of perspective. Only by maintaining some distance would I be able to help the organization and him in his role.

He did not know what he wanted to do. He was still very confused, struggling with the physical and psychological consequences of his illness and with the unbearable prospect of his imminent death, still young. He was also very concerned about the impact on the adolescents of his death as head of the unit.

During that session I let him express his concerns and his confusion aloud with me, without taking any particular direction. Meanwhile, I was trying to keep alive within myself a dialogue between his needs and the unit's needs, between his perspective and other people's views. I was struggling to resist being drawn too much into identifying with, and being affected by, what was happening to this man of my generation, whom I liked, and who had similar values and beliefs to mine.

Transition and regrouping

Rob was struggling with the psychological and physical impact of his illness, the seriousness of which only a few senior staff were aware. His wish to remain part of Sage House was strong and his difficulty in letting go impaired his and his staff's ability to make decisions about the future of the unit. The management of the Rainbow organization finally decided, under some pressure from Sage House senior staff, to appoint an acting director.

I was aware of the negotiations and that the candidate was friendly with Rob and had expressed an interest in Sage House for a number of years. I was hopeful that a new head could give Sage House the stability so badly needed by its staff and residents, but I was also worried about the fragility of this transition and the potential risks of a misalliance.

When John, the new acting director, arrived, the feelings of relief and hope for the future were mixed with a growing idealization of the previous director. The thought of someone new, who brought new ideas and new life, was perceived as an almost unbearable threat to the old order. The staff, who had been bravely holding the organization together, seemed to have partly lost their sense of purpose and worth. Rob's illness became an excuse not to examine their current feelings, thoughts and projects. The arrival of the 'step-parent' had shaken and threatened their transitional system and their sense of value.

It was as if the eldest children were rebelling against the new parent, who seemed, by his presence, to eradicate and deny their plans and past successes.

From personal grief to organizational grief

As a consultant to the senior staff, to the director and to the acting director, I was trying to focus on the entire organization, asking myself what was the best approach for the unit as a whole, rather than for one of its parts. I needed to act as a bridge between present, past and future. Never before had I felt that my role was so central in holding the whole organization in my mind, despite the pressure to take only one point of view. It was also the first time I had to face, in such a direct and powerful way, issues of death, sorrow and hope.

I was working from a *triangular perspective* – a constant internal dialogue between the different parts. At one end, there was the director with his illness and fragility and his difficulty in letting go of his position at Sage House. At the other were the senior staff, with their mixed feelings of sorrow, anger and compassion and desire for life and development. In the middle there was the new director with his expectations and desires, having to deal with Rob's shadow within the unit's 'mind'.

The structure of my intervention reflected this triangular situation. I had meetings with Rob and his deputy, Jane, to help them come to terms with what was happening and negotiate together the best solution for Rob, in the context of the future planning for Sage House, namely how and when should he leave.

In parallel, I met with the senior staff and the acting director, providing a space where they could start to negotiate with each other about their new roles, different responsibilities and their vision for Sage House.

Despite my efforts, the three organizational components never met together, although I continued to carry the three components firmly in my mind. When I met with Rob and Jane, I was constantly thinking of the rest of the unit and the need to find a way forward that would allow the young people and the staff to feel held and contained. Jane, for example, felt at times quite overwhelmed with sorrow for Rob and appeared to hesitate in asking him to make a decision about his retirement. I felt I had to help them to confront the consequences of delaying such a decision. Postponing Rob's formal departure from the organization would have meant disempowering the new director, freezing and putting on hold some important developments. Yet, if Rob had retired too suddenly and with little preparation, the strain and the sense of guilt amongst the staff would have been immense and Rob would have probably felt rejected and treated unfairly.

For the senior staff, listening to and sharing the acting director's ideas and hopes for the unit was unbearable, until, with my help, they started to recognize their feelings of loss for Rob. They also began to acknowledge their criticism of him and some of the things he was unable to offer, which had been holding Sage House back. Talking about their underlying feelings, putting together the different parts of their experience and their history, and dealing with the internal grief and sadness for the loss of their leader, gave the senior staff an opportunity to start a new and healthier stage. At the same time, by allowing themselves and each other to be more objective about Rob's contribution, the acting director was given 'permission' to begin to assert his leadership.

Part of the work was to share some of these private feelings with others, which became part of the organizational learning and culture. When these thoughts and emotions were out in the open, they could be looked at and related to other points of view, feelings and thoughts, allowing both the individuals and the unit as a whole to identify and work through some crucial issues.

I encouraged the staff to relate their private emotions to their roles, just as I had done. Everything experienced as private was in reality important material for their organizational life. What, at times, felt secondary or irrelevant was often key to understanding an important aspect of the process going on within Sage House. They were now gradually moving *from private grief to organizational grief.*

Peter Marris points out that grief is:

> the expression of a profound conflict between contradictory impulses, – to consolidate all that is still valuable from the past, and preserve it from loss; and at the same time, to re-establish a meaningful pattern of relationships, in which the loss is accepted.
>
> (Marris, 1993, p. 31)

As Marris says, people's ability to articulate the process of grieving, re-establishing a sense of what has been lost, can give meaning to the present and make space for change.

The consultant role

Consulting at different levels of an organization, holding information from different groups and individuals, and connecting crucial material without breaking confidentiality present a great challenge for the consultant. The boundaries of consulting to an organization cannot be clearly defined because they continue to be renegotiated throughout the process of consultation.

In the case of Sage House, it was essential to maintain an internal dialogue between the different dimensions involved, but also to mirror them in the structure of my intervention. I had to give a different space and setting to the various people in the organization so that they could work on their difficulties with each other and thus become able to interrelate and function in a productive way.

I was trying to create for myself what Britton calls a 'third position' – 'a capacity for seeing ourselves in interactions with others and for entertaining another point of view whilst retaining our own, for reflecting on ourselves whilst being ourselves' (Britton, 1989, p. 87).

Being constantly in touch with my function and role within Sage House helped me to allow greater flexibility in the external boundaries of my intervention. I was able to be open and receptive to different needs and circumstances when I could hold on to the internal recognition of my role and function. Working with the majority of the staff within the House was a great help; it was a strong reminder that my loyalty was to the whole staff group and not to one or two components. Finally, my identification with the *task itself – the 'ultimate client'* – enabled me to maintain some detachment throughout my intervention.

What is confidential to the individual and what is confidential to the organization? How does one make a distinction between what is professional and what is personal?

An example of this was the secrecy about Rob's illness, which, at the beginning, I regarded mainly as being highly confidential information. Being one the first people connected to Sage House to know about the seriousness of his illness, I experienced an odd sense of privilege at being party to this private information; yet at the same time the knowledge interfered with my ability to maintain a sense of perspective. I wondered to what extent I was protecting myself from the difficulties of challenging this secrecy and helping Rob to be more open, so that Sage House and its staff could be prepared for his departure and consequently more empowered in their roles. At the beginning, some secrecy was required to allow us time to think and work through the initial impact of the news for Rob and others, but later it became vital to involve other people.

How can the consultant detect whether or not she has lost her critical edge?

This dilemma is implicit in any consultancy work, but it becomes crucial in situations of personal tragedy combined with organizational transition and change.

Fundamental to a system-psychodynamic approach to consultancy is the ability to be open to the experience and projections of the people we are consulting. This often implies experiencing very uncomfortable feelings. As Obholzer says:

> ... the counter-transference (is) by far the most useful device ever for 'lowering oneself' into the institutional process *cum* miasma (... 'infectious or noxious emanation') ... it is a device that's always in play – it is merely a question of whether we wish to pay any attention to it, or not.
>
> (Obholzer, 2003, p. 160)

Staying with the situation, bearing the pain and anxiety of 'getting nowhere', without forgetting the need to create organizational structures and framework, is essential to this approach.

As a consultant, your familiarity with and loyalty to a project, after having been involved in it for a number of years, can impinge upon or endanger your capacity to maintain a sense of perspective. It is as if one becomes part of an 'extended family' and can lose one's critical edge under the pressure to become part of the system. Or one can sometimes experience a divided loyalty between an individual one is close to and the organization as a whole. It can be argued that as soon as you cross a boundary you lose your capacity to be completely objective. Being part of the environment and involved with different members of the organization has an incredibly powerful effect.

Dependency is an inevitable part of a consultant's role. The challenge is, as Eric Miller points out, how to respond to dependency needs without creating a dependent organization (Miller, 1993). The attraction of having people dependent on you is strong: it gives an imaginary power and certainty to the role of the organizational consultant, which is, as I see it, relatively new, 'on the boundary between craft and profession' (Miller, 1993).

The senior staff at Sage House dealt with it by not sending me a contract for months and keeping me waiting with regard to further consultancy in the future. I kept reminding them, but I somehow accepted that they were not going to do it. Looking back, I think I was protecting a very delicate, dependent relationship which could not be publicly acknowledged.

I obviously understood that the staff were constantly dealing with the failed dependency of the young people in their care, with their unfulfilled needs and with the task of helping them through the experience of having a positive dependent relationship with the unit in order to gain some skills and internal strength so they could go on to lead autonomous lives.

Rob's increasing openness about his illness, his trust in his colleagues and in myself, and his acceptance of the need to let go of his position allowed other people to contribute to the survival and the development of Sage House. Giving space to others also allowed him to have enough space for himself to make the most of his last months and to prepare for his death.

When I originally wrote the first draft of this chapter, after Rob's death, I wondered if I was exploiting his illness for my professional gains. On reflection I realized that my concerns mirrored some of the feelings the staff were experiencing when they took over responsibility for the unit from Rob. As with many deaths, there is the wish, or hunger, for material and psychological inheritance, which, I think, also offers some protection from the feelings of emptiness and hopelessness that death brings.

3   Organizational and personal shame

The devastating effect of feeling a failure or being exposed as one

It happened to me: the experience of shame after I was quite brutally dropped from teaching on a leadership course. Though the whole incident was unfair and badly managed, still I felt ashamed and exposed. Since then, I became increasingly tuned in to the emotional consequences of shame in the working environment.

The following examples describe the powerful emotions that the feeling of failure can evoke and how these emotions link to individual vulnerabilities and disruptive organizational dynamics.

Lack of trust

Martin, a head nurse, was escorted out of his hospital. He was denied access to his computer and suspended from his duties with immediate effect. He felt devastated and ashamed: his whole career was on the line. His mistake and lapse of judgement didn't seem to match the severity of the penalty.

Martin had a difficult relation with Emma, his boss. He felt unsupported and criticized by her. The situation with Emma had deteriorated in the last year: they rarely met for supervision sessions and she had been quite critical of him in front of senior staff at the hospital. Martin's response to this situation was withdrawal and avoidance. He now experienced any communication with Emma as interference or criticism. He concentrated on his clinical work and became less involved with his duties as a manager.

There had been instances of deaths and serious medical complications as a result of poor practice in a number of hospitals. Martin's area of work, acute medicine, had increasingly become the focus of attention both inside and outside the hospital, and had inevitably absorbed some of the anxiety around death on behalf of the whole institution. Martin was feeling more and more isolated and was thinking of looking for another job.

A colleague from a different hospital invited him to give a talk at a conference abroad. After some consideration, Martin decided to do it in a private capacity. He didn't tell his boss – he was angry with her and also fearful she would block this initiative, even if he was doing it in his own time. However, he also forgot to book his leave for the days of the conference. Emma eventually found out and, while Martin was away, started a fraud investigation in the belief that he had carried out a private assignment during his hospital hours. By the time Martin came back, Emma had already formed a strong view against him and she suspended him with immediate effect.

Lohmer and Lazar talk about trust as a fundamental requirement for cooperation in organizations, but they also point out that trust implies risk, 'placing our confidence in the other'. They talk of 'active trust', based on the capacity of an institution to be open, where the relationships between the different players require transparency and participation on all levels. This often doesn't happen: the anxiety radiating from the organizational task frequently leads to a *dynamic of mistrust* that 'jeopardizes the possibilities of containment of fears and tensions within the organizations' (Lohmer and Lazar, 2006, p. 48).

In Martin's example, the challenges of his working environment had resulted in quite a paranoid atmosphere, where the level of anxiety made him retreat into his own position rather than look for help and understanding from his colleagues and manager. It was very distressing for Martin to face the possibility of losing his job, after years of good clinical work and strong commitment to the organization. It was a traumatic experience.

Trauma can be seen as an attack on attachment, provoking a sense of persecution and mistrust:

> A traumatic event is not simply understood as an external experience, a random life incident superimposed on an individual. Instead it is reinterpreted in the mind in terms of a relationship with an internal object.... In this kind of scenario, an internal sense of goodness and safety is threatened and the individual is left with a feeling of despair that the world is no longer a secure place.
>
> (Levy and Lemma , 2004, pp. 27, 37)

An excessive fear of losing the positive image of oneself is often related to a work setting where difficulties and complex problems are not dealt with in an open way, and where it doesn't feel possible to acknowledge that mistakes are sometimes inevitable and poor performance is not just the responsibility of one or a few individuals. In such a context, relationships among staff tend to be defensive and blaming of each other, hindering the possibility of learning from experience.

Martin's hospital was under a lot of scrutiny: what happened to him mirrored the dynamics of mistrust and criticism the hospital was daily experiencing from the wider context outside the institution.

Am I an impostor?

Joe, a senior executive in a large global company, had enjoyed a good career. He had developed a positive relationship with his boss, who, despite being based in a different country, had always been approachable and supportive.

When his boss retired, Joe was promised a new role that he felt was well earned after many years of hard work and loyal commitment to the organization. His new boss encouraged him to apply for the position, but eventually chose someone else – a younger and less experienced colleague. Joe was devastated. He felt betrayed by his 'work family' and profoundly humiliated in front of his peers.

It was a 'public' humiliation: everyone knew he had applied and he was expecting to get the job. His current role was also going to be made obsolete in the next few months and he now found himself without a clear career future, facing the possibility of redundancy.

Hoggett makes a distinction between depressive shame and paranoid shame:

> Depressive shame is a quite healthy emotion because it might lead us to be disappointed with ourselves and therefore resolved to address our failures and meet our goals and ideals … Paranoid shame might be a much more corrosive feeling of humiliation where one feels just not good enough … all or nothing, where failure means uselessness.
>
> (Hoggett, 2017)

Joe thought his career was now crumbling and he started to doubt his own value and competence. He felt paranoid about his organization, fearing people would find out he wasn't really what they originally thought.

Was he an impostor?

His emotional reactions were clearly linked to a difficult upbringing and inner vulnerability. However, the organizational culture – highly competitive and quite ruthless – contributed to his experience of shame. His failure occurred under the gaze of many of his colleagues, which made his situation even more unbearable.

Fearing the loss of power

Louisa, a senior medical consultant in a large teaching hospital, was accused of bullying behaviour towards a number of the junior staff. The medical director decided not to suspend her and gave her instead a period of leave during which she was to undertake an intensive coaching programme – an opportunity to understand and address her behaviour.

It was a tricky assignment that I took on with some trepidation. I was expecting to meet an angry and possibly quite arrogant consultant. However, in our first meeting, Louisa appeared mainly upset, struggling to come to terms with the way she had been portrayed and experienced by some of the staff at her hospital. She was in shock. She couldn't recognize the person they were describing. Years of excellent clinical practice seemed to have evaporated in the context of these complaints.

Louisa's response to this situation was connected to her experience of her position and role, acquired through a long and challenging training and a successful clinical practice, and it was coloured by an underlying disbelief that her behaviour could be questioned after such a distinguished career.

A sense of entitlement can be linked to a narcissistic position where the individual denies her need for dependence. Losing a sense of an omnipotent self-sufficiency puts the person in touch 'with dependent needy feelings which give rise to anxiety' (Steiner, 2006).

Louisa struggled to acknowledge how profoundly affected she was as a result of the accusations of bullying and how anxious she felt about going back to the hospital and re-engage with the people who have complained about her behaviour.

Recovery from shame

While these clients' responses to shame were all different, they were equally powerful. Their feelings of vulnerability and sense of failure were strongly linked to their personal history and backgrounds.

Both Martin and Joe had complex family backgrounds. Work had provided a refuge where they had escaped their upbringing and had been able to prove their value. However, they had often felt ambivalent about their worth, as if they were still questioning their entitlement and competence. At a deeper level, the 'fall from grace' represented a confirmation of these doubts; it was experienced as a profound trauma, an attack on their primary identity.

In contrast, Louisa struggled to come to terms with the challenge to her well-established position and status – the result of a privileged background and also of dedication and hard work. She felt shaken and humiliated, but her sense of self-worth remained largely intact. Her reaction was also influenced by the organizational response. While Martin was suspended and almost expelled by his organization and Joe spent many months in a marginalized and uncertain position, Louisa was protected from humiliation and given the opportunity to review her behaviour. Louisa's organization offered a more mature response to the situation, possibly also influenced by her seniority and role.

The focus of my work with Martin was on recovering his sense of agency and his capacity to fight back. He was gradually able to move from feeling overwhelmed and hopeless to taking action in order to return to work and recover his reputation. The challenge was for him to recognize his own responsibility in the situation, without taking a victim position and blaming it all on his manager and the organization. When someone has been directly affected by a humiliating experience, the appeal of taking a 'victim' role can be very strong, thereby denying one's own hostility and part in the dynamic.

Joe felt profoundly negative towards his organization. Suddenly his sense of connection and belonging was replaced by anger and resentment. This strong reaction was also linked to his experience of neglect from his own parents. The 'idealized surrogate family' that the company had represented for him for many years had become persecutory and neglectful too. Joe needed to address his dependency towards his organization in order to regain confidence in his own skills and experience. Starting to look outwards and exploring possibilities outside his company helped him to shift his position and to recover some confidence in himself.

Joe didn't leave. He invested a lot of energy in rebranding himself within his organization and managed to find a suitable role where he regained his sense of competence and effectiveness.

Perhaps his strong dependency on the 'surrogate family' prevented him from finding an alternative job in a different company. However, the experience of marginalization and shame helped him to regain a sense of perspective about his organization and acknowledge that he needed to be more open and invested in his life outside the company.

Louisa's consultancy journey was about understanding her behaviour and how she came across to junior and less experienced staff. Her challenge was to be open to reviewing her conduct without using her clinical expertise as a defence or justification for her bullying approach. It wasn't easy for Louisa to put herself in other people's shoes and understand the anxiety behind their behaviour in complex clinical situations. What she feared most was to be looked at with contempt.

I never heard back from Louisa, despite our agreement to a follow-up session. I wondered if the 'narcissistic wound' of having to confront her behaviour and shortcomings was still open: she couldn't face coming back.

★★★

Shame affects both the organization and the individual: it is the possibility of shame that leads organizations to act too quickly and get rid of 'the bad apple' without thinking; and it is the shame of being seen to do something wrong or to be experienced as inadequate that contributes to the collapse of confidence and competence in the individuals involved.

The public nature of working in an organization makes us more exposed to humiliation and vulnerable to shame. The challenge for organizations and individuals is to move from persecutory shame to depressive shame, accepting shame as, at times, an inevitable ingredient of the complexity of organizational life – being able to feel ashamed without collapsing under the scrutiny of other people.

In the examples described, the consultancy input had an important function in restoring some capacity for reflection and a sense of perspective. It helped the individuals concerned to deal with their feelings of guilt and despair and to manage the wish to blame others or give it all up.

4 The grey area

Consulting at the interface between the personal and the professional

The capacity to understand the link between current difficulties at work and our early life experiences can have a transformative effect on our approach to our working lives. In my consultancy practice, I have been struck by the shifts in behaviour and organizational dynamics that such awareness can generate.

Understanding the connection between a current work problem and a dynamic originating in our early years can be difficult. It might challenge a well-established view of ourselves and our defensive structures. However, it can also help unlock new resources, energy and skills that have been obscured and impaired by the shadow of the past.

We might have an emotional sense that a past dynamic influences our behaviour without consciously acknowledging it or knowing what it is – what Bollas described as the 'unthought known' (Bollas, 1987).

Melanie Klein in her seminal paper 'Our adult world and its roots in infancy' talks about the influence of early relationships on adult life and the insights we gain 'into the way our mind, our habits, and our views have been built up from the earliest infantile phantasies, and emotions to the most complex adult manifestations' (Klein, 1959, pp. 14, 18).

I call the zone at the interface between the personal and professional the 'grey area', where our individual characteristics and early relationships play out or get expressed in our work role. Addressing the grey area means understanding these connections and bringing them to the surface. An awareness of these connections can help us to find ways of managing aspects of ourselves that have a negative or disruptive impact on our working lives and can also create opportunities for shifting behaviours belonging to the past that we have felt compelled to repeat – what Freud described as 'repetition compulsion' (Freud, 1920).

Here follow three illustrations of working with clients on the *grey area*. This approach gave these individuals new perspectives and created opportunities for them to make some changes in their work situations.

A lone player: the consequences of losing the familiar

William got in touch with me at a time of great anxiety and distress. He was head of pastoral care and safeguarding at an inner-city university. A few months earlier he had experienced a serious health issue, probably stress related. He was now concerned about both his health and the university's situation.

He felt the leadership team didn't take safeguarding seriously enough. There was an extremely relaxed approach to boundaries – the relationship between students and lecturers was very informal, creating confusion about roles and different responsibilities – and a tendency to turn a blind eye to incidents. He felt very alone in his role and became increasingly apprehensive about the potential risks for staff and students.

William came from a working-class background. The first in his family to go to university, he felt highly motivated to transform his work environment. Passionate about sport and outdoor activities, he loved to tackle a challenge.

However, underneath his competent approach, he felt quite insecure and longed for approval and recognition. His desire to impress and embrace a challenge made him feel over-responsible for his organization. He was slow to involve other people, almost seeing this task as his own personal crusade. His passion and high sense of duty fuelled an 'omnipotent stance', a strong conviction he could overcome all the obstacles that he struggled to manage.

My reaction to William's situation was very strong. Hearing the details of the university environment, its gross lack of staff accountability and loose boundaries – and realizing how stressed he felt, prompted me to suggest he should leave his job, an unusual comment on my part at the beginning of a consultation. I was struck by my quick response, made without much reflection, as if I had in turn taken a safeguarding role towards him, mirroring his sense of urgency and feelings of responsibility.

William did leave his job, but it took him longer than 12 months. He wanted to leave on good terms and to fulfil his own objective of putting 'the house in order'. While he should have left much earlier, given the risks to his health and his state of mind, he was determined to complete a full academic year.

Working with William on the *grey area* meant addressing his need for affirmation and his desire to take up challenges, and trying to understand the dynamics behind these. His determination often made him blind to the risks he was taking and unable to delegate to other people. I wondered if his position in relation to his original family – he was very different from his siblings in many respects – made him act alone, as if he didn't have a family or a team to involve or lean on. Though he felt affection towards his family of origin he didn't belong there anymore.

My response to William was central to the understanding of the dynamics below the presenting issue. The intensity and feeling of responsibility I experienced towards his situation mirrored his powerful sense of duty and accountability. My insights into my own desire to rescue William from his challenging work environment helped me to address his omnipotent wish to 'save' the university at all costs.

Moving away from his family and developing a professional career and a very different lifestyle to his parents and siblings had created an emotional gap for William. He felt different and constantly driven to prove his worth.

There was something fragile about his identity, a lack of grounding and a sense of having lost 'his tribe'.

Miller talks of the 'paradoxes inherent in our psychosocial being ... the coexistence of the drive to be separate and autonomous and the need to be attached, to belong' (Miller, 1999, p. 99). This tension was particularly complex for William, who constantly pursued his difference, while yearning for belonging.

In the next example, differently from William, my client had escaped from his 'tribe' and original context and struggled with issues of attachment and belonging.

Needing to belong: the risk of institutionalization

George had a complicated past. His parents divorced when he was very young and his father soon disappeared from his life. Brought up by a controlling and anxious mother, he couldn't wait to leave home. University 'saved' him. He did well and managed to find an interesting position in a large technical company, straight after graduation. The organization became his family.

George progressed well over the years and became established as a highly organized and very technically competent manager. He came to coaching at a time when he felt quite stuck and unable to progress further. It became clear that his 'attachment' to the organization was deeply rooted in his problematic attachment to his own family. It was difficult for George to look at his role and his organization from an objective perspective – he felt too close.

It came as a great shock to learn a few months later that George's role had been made redundant. He felt deeply affected and betrayed by the organization as a result.

My earlier work with George on the *grey area* was to connect his need for attachment with his relationship to the organization. I had often felt overwhelmed by the amount of technical details he presented about his job, as well as quite disconnected from his experience, as if there were a missing connection between us. George struggled to articulate his feelings, unless he was under a lot of stress.

On this occasion, when his job was made obsolete, I managed to engage with him differently. His raw feelings of betrayal and sadness couldn't be contained. I was able to connect with his difficulties in more depth.

For over 20 years the organization had been his 'home'. He couldn't imagine working in a different place and, even more than this, having his competence recognized somewhere else. George had lost his sense of identity as a 'separate' professional with skills transferable to other institutions.

The anger towards his neglectful father and controlling mother was unconsciously shifted onto the organization. His 'organizational family' had abandoned him and he felt resentful and profoundly sad. It was as if he didn't know who he was anymore, having lost his sense of identity with the job:

> ... the childhood experience of attachment influences the sense of security, the pain, serenity or vulnerability with which someone apprehends the world in general and so the resilience of their underlying emotional and purposive structure in the face of loss.
>
> (Marris, 1996, p. 119)

George's struggle to cope with a difficult but manageable situation and his excessive dependence on his organization demonstrated the consequence of a disturbed early attachment.

It took time to help him to look at his situation in a more objective way – he hadn't been fired and there were still other opportunities in the organization – and to relate his extreme reaction to his family background. Through his work with me, he was able to make some connections between his response to the organizational issue and his need for the reliable and positive attachment that he had never experienced when young. We gradually managed to explore different options, including looking at other organizations and considering retraining.

Attachment is also a theme in the following example, where 'separation distress' at an early age might have contributed to some difficulties in the work place.

Feeling entitled: locked in a closed system

Martha, a successful partner in a law firm, was accused of harassment by some of her junior and administrative staff.

This came as a complete shock to her. Although very demanding, she felt she took a fair approach to her team. However, the head of human resources strongly recommended that she had some coaching. She wasn't given the choice to turn it down.

I was concerned that Martha, a busy high flier, would be annoyed at having to go through this process. I was worried I would be dismissed as an unwelcome distraction from her hectic schedule.

To my surprise, Martha appeared anxious and hurt. She clearly had been very upset by the harassment allegations and she became quite tearful during the session. She couldn't see herself as a bully, but she understood she could intimidate people. Her main focus was providing excellent service to her clients. The team around her was not a priority. She acknowledged she didn't think much of people who didn't perform well.

Coming from a family of lawyers, law had been an obvious career choice for her. After a tough training, she expected a lot from herself, but also from other people. And, as a woman, she had had to fight extra hard for respect and authority.

With Martha, the work on the *grey area* was to connect her upbringing, her privileged education and her understanding of her partner role with the way she behaved in the work place. I was highly aware of representing the 'medicine' she had to swallow; I wanted to be experienced by her as open minded and not judgemental. I was particularly careful when phrasing my questions and comments for fear of provoking a defensive or hostile reaction.

An unconscious feeling of entitlement coloured Martha's practice and made her quite unaware of the people around her and of their struggles.

I felt I needed to widen her perspective, helping her to understand the world 'from the other side'. Her professional excellence wasn't enough to lead her team successfully; she needed to learn how to connect and understand their difficulties in coping with the challenges of demanding and difficult clients.

Her response was mixed. She struggled to empathize with people who performed poorly and to imagine ways of dealing with them differently. However, when I encouraged her to share critical incidents and examples from her practice, she started to broaden her view and see how her behaviour, which was mainly focused on technical issues and performance, was making some members of her team anxious and could also lead to poor performance.

I asked her about her family. She lit up and looked quite different, talking about her adolescent children and the challenges and pleasures of being a parent, saying, 'The people who say I am a bully should see how my daughter treats me!' It appeared that she behaved quite differently at home, being very encouraging of her children and trying hard not to show disappointment in their behaviour. I commented on how she needed to transfer some of the emotional capacity she clearly showed in her family life to the world of work.

Her strict training, where keeping a distance was seen as a positive thing, the influence of her father, an authoritative old school barrister, and her boarding-school background had given her an armour that possibly helped in some aspects of her practice, but had a negative impact on her role as a team leader, making her too critical, demanding and narrowly focused.

I wondered if this contrasting behaviour at work and at home was partly related to her boarding-school experience and early separation from her family, indicating an internalized split between tasks and emotions that had been developed as a defensive reaction against loss and loneliness: 'separation distress' in the absence of the attachment figures (Bowlby, 1969).

By encouraging Martha to transfer some of her emotional intelligence from the family context to a work setting, I was hoping to lessen this split and to make her realize she was capable of tuning in with the emotional climate of her work environment.

★★★

As Klein rightly states, our adult experience is rooted in our early years. Our upbringing and relevant experiences are always 'present' in our working lives – they are our 'shadow'. They motivate our choices and fuel our desire for certain professions and areas of work.

Having an awareness and understanding of the personal dimensions and dynamics we bring to our work situations can moderate the effect of the difficulties originating in the past and help us to manage our roles in a more insightful and effective way.

In the examples I have described, the individuals were all struggling, partly unconsciously, with unexamined complexities in their personal lives that were having a powerful impact on their work situations.

Through a process of co-creation, the consultancy sessions helped my clients to cast a light on shadow areas in their lives and make some meaningful connections between their past childhood experiences and present circumstances (Cardona and Damon, 2019).

The relationship between consultant and client is key to creating a reflective space where this exploration can take place, in a setting where trust can be developed and uncertainty tolerated (see Chapters 2 and 10). 'Freud was clear … when he said that insight alone is not enough change. Real change is brought about by "working through", a process of re-learning at a deeply emotional level' (Long, 2015, p. 42).

5 The challenge of succession
Leadership dynamics and conflicts in different contexts

The process of succession is always challenging. In families, the imminent death of the parents can cast a shadow over family dynamics and strongly affect relationships. Shakespeare's tragedy *King Lear* provides an extreme example of how unmet expectations, greed and ambition can precipitate the disintegration of a family.

Successions in organizations are equally complex. Organizations don't usually pay enough attention to the dynamics of succession and to the powerful emotions affecting the experience of the people involved. For example, the departing leader might feel pushed out and unwanted. The staff left behind might feel abandoned, experiencing a loss of protection and guidance. The incoming leader might fear people's judgement and comparisons, and struggle to prove his or her difference and value. I have described in Chapter 2 the challenges faced by the acting director of Sage House and how feelings of hope for the future were mixed with feelings of guilt and idealization of the previous director.

These primitive emotions may remain unconscious and unacknowledged. As a consequence, feelings can get displaced or acted out into disruptive dynamics, leading to difficult and painful succession processes.

An example of a troubled succession took place at the National Theatre, when it was led from 1963 to 1973 by the great actor and director Laurence Olivier. His poor health and a series of failures at the new theatre led the board to look for a new director. The succession process was apparently managed behind his back, with his successor, Peter Hall, sworn to secrecy. In the end, 'Olivier was confronted with a *fait accompli* and felt he had been stitched up …' His wife, in a BBC documentary, spoke of 'treachery of the highest order' (Billington, 2013).

This example illustrates some of the dynamics at the core the succession process: the difficulties of facing the end of an era and the guilt associated with the responsibility of letting the old leader go. It must have felt particularly challenging and distressing to 'sack' Olivier, one of the most celebrated actors of our time and a renowned international figure. These difficult and, possibly, unbearable feelings created the conditions for 'acting out' – the exclusion of Olivier from the succession process, as a defence against the anxiety of confronting his likely disappointment and anger, and because of the apprehension around fully embracing the need for change in the National Theatre. This dynamic is not unusual; succession can stir up very raw and disruptive emotions.

Consultancy during the succession process can create opportunities for understanding the experiences of the people involved and help them to acknowledge the inevitability of some of these feelings, allowing individuals to take a clearer ownership of their situation and encouraging organizations to develop transitional systems to support this process.

Killing the father

The desire to take the parents' place is complex, as is the desire to replace the leader. They can be coloured by feelings of guilt, impatience, frustration and anger.

In the Oedipus myth, King Laius hears a prediction that his son Oedipus will kill him and marry his mother. In response to this prediction, Laius arranges the murder of his son. However, Oedipus survives. As we know from the story, he will eventually fulfil the oracle's prophecy. This myth is a powerful reminder of our unconscious desire 'to kill' our parents and the inevitability of metaphorically having to do so, in order to gain maturity and independence.

Winnicott talks of the adolescent's need to 'kill' the father, as part of his maturational process (Winnicott, 1969). However, the guilt associated with the desire to take the parents' place is one of the main motivations behind messy and distressing succession processes, as the next example shows.

★★★

Chris wanted the top job. He was bright, competent and well respected. He had risen very rapidly through the ranks of his organization, a successful international think tank. A highly ambitious Oxbridge graduate, he had already gained a place in the senior executive team. He expressed great admiration for the director, Alan, who had been a role model and a source of encouragement to him since he had joined the company.

However, Chris was beginning to feel uneasy about Alan's authoritarian leadership style and he was aware of a growing criticism of Alan's leadership within the organization and at board level. When a coup was organized to oust the director by some key board members, Chris didn't react. He was too invested in developing his own career to risk his reputation to protect his boss. He subsequently became the next director, quite young for such a senior position.

In my role as consultant to the executive team, I felt fairly powerless and I was unable to make any effective interventions. Towards the very end, Alan confided in me about the attacks that had been made on him and his awareness of a plot against him. He was angry, humiliated and perhaps for the first time, a bit scared. I could see how he had brought some of the attacks upon himself. His rather arrogant and autocratic approach, his contempt for many of his colleagues and also his success and charisma, made him a likely target for attack.

However, such a difficult ending could have been avoided if Chris and other members of the executive team had taken a more constructive role in managing the succession. Yet I could sense how Chris, maybe not completely consciously, would see the benefit of 'killing the father' instead of engaging in a lengthy and complex succession process.

As Alan left, I was also 'expelled', as a potential reminder of his reign and of the nasty coup that got rid of him.

The painful feelings connected with ending and death, the difficulty of letting go of power and authority, and the greed and desire to take the 'father's place' can mobilize disruptive dynamics, preventing the possibility of a more thoughtful and meaningful transition (see also Chapter 2).

My own relationship with the executive team was also significant in what happened. I was tolerated, but never fully accepted – the 'outsider' perceived with suspicion and ambivalence. Their relationship with me mirrored their own difficult relationship with the outside world and their sense of often being misunderstood and misrepresented when trying to represent controversial views. I never felt fully grounded in this intervention, as if my difference and my consultancy stance were almost intolerable and prevented a full engagement between us. Therefore, it wasn't surprising not to be asked back by the new leadership.

Paradoxically, I had wanted to make the organization more open and transparent internally. I had tried to encourage the executive team and the director to share some of their discontent and differences (discussed in the individual coaching sessions) in the group work. It felt challenging, as people were extremely invested in presenting an image of efficiency and competence to each other, which meant that they struggled to show difficulties and vulnerabilities.

The process of succession created a stage for acting out some of those dynamics – a 'perfect storm'. The criticism, dissatisfaction and complex feelings towards the director that people were unable to discuss openly, produced the background for his ejection.

The next example explores a different dynamic in succession, where a family business becomes a battleground for siblings looking for love and attention from their parents.

Fighting for parental love

The three children of a successful entrepreneur were very critical of each other's characters and extremely competitive about their different roles within the family company.

The father, in his mid-seventies, was still in control of the business and was ambivalent about letting go of his CEO position. A self-made man, he had created a successful IT company in a niche market.

His son, Henry, was initially seen as the likely 'heir'. The first-born, male and with an IT degree, he was invested with great responsibility from an earlier age. However, the father became disappointed with his performance and Henry didn't progress far within the company.

The middle daughter, Rona, was bright and creative, and didn't want anything to do with the company. She went travelling and then started to work in an art gallery. A few years later, feeling disappointed with the art world, she joined the company, taking up a role in the HR department. Olivia, the youngest daughter, joined the company at a later stage; she seemed to find a good fit with a role in finance and was starting to gain a positive feedback within the organization.

The three siblings realized that their relationships with each other were getting out control and affecting their private lives as well as their business. It was at this point that they decided to approach me for some consultancy input. The consultancy focused on both their private roles in the family and on their work roles in the business. It was a painful journey.

Though the father had a controlling position within the company and was very reluctant to let go of his power within the business, the main obstacle to an effective succession plan was the siblings' rivalry and their difficult relationships with each other.

Both parents had been very involved with their own work and didn't have much time for family life. They were hoping the children would take significant roles within the business, and had high expectations about their contribution. The siblings therefore experienced both pressure and disappointment from their parents. The business became the battleground for their parents' love.

Through the consultancy process, the siblings were able to start making a distinction between their family roles and their professional roles, and to address some of the early dynamics that had influenced their later experience. The focus was on the interface between the family system and business system. The siblings were longing for recognition and appreciation, though their competitive dynamics and their grievances generated a sense of frustration and disappointment in each other and in their parents.

Creating opportunities for dialogue and revisiting critical incidents in their upbringing and their involvement in the family business helped them to develop some trust in each other. Through the experience of a shared reflective space and the full attention and focus of a consultant 'parental figure', they were able to build stronger connections and become more tolerant of each other's shortcomings.

The siblings then became capable of initiating the succession process and engaging with their parents about their desires for the company and for themselves in an open way. It finally seemed possible to start the transition from *parental power* to *sibling power* (Cardona and Raffaelli, 2016). The dynamic of succession became possible only when they started to cooperate with each other and created a '*sibling we identity*' (Coles, 2003), 'a crucial emotional factor in the establishment of a strategic space' (Osnes, 2014, p. 100).

Sibling power

In the following example, the planned retirement of a leader opened up the opportunity to develop a different kind of leadership. Yet the transition from a charismatic leadership to a 'sibling/lateral leadership' presented numerous challenges, despite a well-thought-out transitional phase, strongly supported by the departing leader. Armstrong defines 'lateral relations' as: 'a relation between collaborating persons, role holders, groups or team, that is unmediated by any actual or assumed hierarchical authority' (Armstrong, 2007, p. 194).

Judith had been the clinical head of an influential mental health charity for a number of years. When she took up her role the charity was in decline, despite a distinguished background in innovative research and practice. She was able to place the organization's future on a more secure footing and bring new energy into the senior team and the board. Despite the reduction of staff and resources, the senior team could now see the relevance of their organization and its potential role in the wider environment.

The consultancy started at a time of significant generational change, with the succession from the older generation to a younger and new senior team. Judith had already planned her retirement in a year's time and a few other key people were also planning to leave. My role was to help the organization through this transitional period and prepare the team for change and development.

Despite her good intentions, Judith struggled to develop confidence in the senior team. She could see how some members were struggling to take up their authority and how others were highly competitive with each other. The senior team was still very dependent on her for directions and vision.

The clock was ticking …

There were differences of approach among the members of the team and competition for resources and space. However, there was also a real desire to find ways of working together. Judith, with her vision and focus, had been able to hold the whole organization in mind and had provided a clear reference point for the staff. Inevitably, it was easier and more containing to rely on one identifiable leader than on a group.

The challenge was to develop the senior team into a 'leadership team' – a team able to share with each other and to confront each other, as well as being capable of providing a cohesive environment for the whole organization. However, the pressures and concerns arising from their different areas of responsibility were affecting their focus, preventing the group from addressing the organization's core issues and dynamics.

With my help, the team gradually built 'a collective space' where they addressed their conflicting agendas and diverse views, and managed the potential splits between the different parts of the organizational system.

The group developed substantially, allowing Judith to leave with enough confidence in the organization's future. The 'sibling/lateral leadership' seemed sufficiently robust to take the organization forward.

★★★

The concept of siblings has been neglected in psychoanalytic literature. Freud thought that sibling relationships were coloured by hostility and primitive hatred. Other authors recognize the positive influence siblings have in our development and internal world:

> We need our siblings and peers to help us get away from our parents and teach us how to relate in a different way ... The feelings we have towards our siblings have an importance place in the complexity of our emotional life.
>
> (Coles, 2003, p. 2)

Sibling relationships provide the blueprint for developing and sustaining relationships and can provide mirroring, companionship, continuity and love (Silverstone, 2006).

A lateral leadership creates a horizontal system that can be more effective than a hierarchical–vertical paradigm. It can also represent a better fit with today's organizational environments and the new emerging structures in the work place.

Armstrong talks of the difficulty of reconciling the 'sense of sameness with the acknowledgement of differences' – differences that can provoke feelings of rivalry, envy, guilt and shame. A lateral leadership entails the development of a shared 'boundary of identity' that 'may require putting in question or suspending just those pre-existing boundaries of identity that mark out and serve to define the differences' (Armstrong, 2007).

Dismissal

Once the succession process had started, I didn't carry on working with any of the organizations I have described. The think tank didn't get in touch after their former leader Alan's departure, the family business promised regular updates that never happened and the mental health charity kept postponing follow-up meetings.

It might have been right not to involve me anymore – a result of the need for change and the desire to move on. I wonder if I would have represented the older generation too much, even if I had engaged with both the older and the new emerging leadership.

Yet my implicit 'dismissal' could also be linked with the strong feelings of guilt associated with taking the parents' place and the denial of the experience of loss. As consultant to that process, I became a reminder of a particular challenging time that people wanted to put behind them. The new leadership didn't want to risk being affected by the powerful and potentially overwhelming feelings that such challenging times entail.

6 The manager's most precious skill★

The capacity to be 'psychologically present'

'I woke up at four this morning. I was concerned about the ward. There were only five staff to look after fourteen patients. Two of the patients are potentially suicidal and require special attention. One of the staff on the night shift cancelled at the last minute and I made the decision not to call in an extra person. I felt the pressure of keeping the money down and I didn't want to call in agency staff, because usually they do very little. I don't want the staff to get into the habit of using an agency and there were two students who could have helped in case of serious acting out.'

Anne, an experienced manager of an acute psychiatric ward, was worried because that day she had had to dash off at five. She explained to me that she had not had enough time to go through all the cases in depth and was concerned that she might have missed some clues concerning potential risks.

Is Anne's behaviour a sign of stress or an indication that she was psychologically in touch with her staff?

I think that Anne, despite leaving the ward at five, remained 'psychologically present'; she maintained a connection with her team that made her wake up early the next morning to check the situation. She was able to get on with her life without abandoning her responsibility to the ward.

In my experience, the manager's ability to be psychologically present has increasingly become a key ingredient in the functioning, development and stability of staff.

What is psychological presence?

In an organizational climate of constant change, mergers and restructuring, where organizations are no longer able to provide a safe psychological container for their employees, the manager's capacity to be fully there becomes an essential element for stability and growth.

William Khan has developed the concept of psychological presence as 'the experiential state accompanying the behaviours of personally engaged role performance' (Khan, 1992, p. 331). Khan links this 'personal engagement' with the authenticity of working with one's real emotions. He identifies three main essential conditions for being psychologically present:

1   not being too preoccupied with one's own issues,
2   being involved in a meaningful task,
3   feeling safe enough to 'employ the self without the fear of negative consequences'.

(p. 333)

The degree to which individuals experience these three conditions determines how psychologically present and engaged they can be in some work situations. As Miller (1999) points out, even if all three conditions are met, the individual has to choose to be psychologically present. Choice becomes a crucial element. He argues that there are 'good reasons for moving towards organizational forms that give full recognition to people as autonomous, choice-making individuals as opposed to interchangeable objects', and identifies that what is missing in many organizations is 'a structure that recognizes that "human resources" have a stake in the larger system, and individual contributions to make to it, that go beyond the work-roles' (p. 109).

Management and the parental function

There are many useful comparisons that can be made between the role of management and that of parenting. Parents, and particularly mothers, often struggle with the difficulty of keeping the child in mind and being able to postpone or put on hold their own priorities in order to concentrate on their children's needs, without giving up their adult world and their focus on reality. In a world which puts an ever-increasing pressure on parents to perform multiple roles – to have a successful career, to look fit and young, and to be active and proactive parents – it becomes increasingly difficult to be psychologically there for our children. Career and financial preoccupations, practical pressures and household tasks can take parents away from an essential psychological presence. Our children, overfed and 'over-gadgetted', are often left to their own devices when it comes to coping with some of the emotional ups and downs of growing up.

In our society, there are now more permeable boundaries between the world of adults and the world of children, and this can create the illusory feeling of a peer relationship between parents and children, and a denial of the reality of the differences in responsibility and need for a degree of dependence. These two tendencies – 'the over-preoccupied' parents and the 'parent-peer mentality' – can take away the essential ingredients of psychological presence: the capacity to listen and to be fully in touch with the emotional lives of our children.

I would argue that these two tendencies in the parent–child relationship are also present in the manager–staff relationship. The world of work has become increasingly complex and turbulent: managers often have to deal with conflicting demands. They are under great pressure to solve practical problems, respond to financial crises and implement changes. They can also minimize the differences in roles and responsibilities and neglect their staff's need for dependence. Wesley Carr (2001) makes an interesting distinction between dependence and dependency: 'Dependent existence is neither good nor bad: it simply "is". This state we may call "dependence"' (p. 50). We vary in relation to it from birth, one moment regressing, and the next fiercely wanting to stand on our own feet. Through this behaviour we work out various dependent relationships – and that is how we learn their worth.

Dependency refers to the 'unconscious surrender of authority' and auto-nomy, when people become anxious about survival and become 'unthink-ingly dependent' (p. 51). Managers have to understand and manage this distinction, and be able to respond to their staff's need for dependence without encouraging a dependency culture.

The following example demonstrates what I mean.

Linda did not come from the ranks. She had been a successful general manager who had been promoted to a senior position in a newly formed mental health trust. She was well aware of not having earned her position through clinical work with clients and she was very keen to win the trust of the staff she managed.

However, she had a relentless schedule. Linda knew that she should have been more present at floor level, but often felt too busy to spend time with her staff. After a recent visit to a team, she reflected on her experience: 'If I go "down" people can be quite hostile and not very welcoming, but I realize afterwards that I get less complaints from the staff.'

In parental terms, this seems to link with the idea that often 'doing' things for the children is not enough. One needs to be available and visible, particularly in adolescence when young people can seem hostile or indifferent to parental involvement but still need the presence, the concern and the control of their parents. A major difficulty for parents and managers in remaining present and available is being in a context in which their presence is often not acknowledged, or is even opposed, and to still be able to recognize the need for dependence. Unresponsive or antagonistic staff can frustrate or depress the manager, who may react by retreating into other business and becoming increasingly remote.

What are the challenges to the manager's capacity to be psychologically present?

External and internal factors, personal characteristics and style of working can put pressure on, or diminish, the manager's capacity to be psychologically present. Organizational changes, threats to a well-established way of working, the ambition to maintain clinical excellence, the seduction of the political debate, or the desire to rescue every situation can interfere with the manag-er's capacity to be psychologically available to his/her staff.

Hirschhorn, in his book *Reworking Authority* (1997), talks about the need for staff today to become more resourceful psychologically. The relaxing of hierarchies creates greater freedom to negotiate roles and express one's individual talents: 'Individuals rely more on their personal authority – they bring more of themselves, their skills, ideas, feelings and values' (p. 1). Relationships are more personalized and open, but there is a risk of provoking feelings that people cannot contain. This culture of openness makes people more receptive to the ideas, thoughts and feelings of others, but it requires more sophisticated and different ways of providing containment. Some managers can go too far in trying to make people happy. As a result, they can experience incompetence and negative behaviour in their staff as their own failure.

Sam had successfully made a transition from a senior position in the commercial sector to a leading role in the voluntary sector. He explained:

> In my previous job, which was a big one – I was on the board and there were many departments – it took me a long time to realize that I needed to spend 70 to 80 per cent of my time with people. I had to be available for people to drop in and see me. If you were inflexible and said, 'I can't see you for the next three or four days,' you would be creating big problems for the future. The whole thing of being available for people without being abused is incredibly difficult to manage.
>
> There was someone who worked here: he resigned after he had been sick for a long time and all of a sudden, out of the blue, he takes me to an industrial tribunal for constructive dismissal. I did know that he was unhappyish and during the appraisal process I really tried to do something about it. I don't like having unhappy people. I go too far in trying to make them happy.
>
> That is where I went wrong. I believed that everything was salvageable – and it wasn't. The organization was changing quite rapidly and I didn't think he had the competence to deal with it; he was living in the past. Trying to move him forward was quite difficult. I did think he wanted to leave, but I didn't want him to leave, I thought it would be a failure.

In situations like this, a culture of 'positiveness' becomes a barrier to being psychologically present, and is used as a shield against the fear of negative projections. This approach can be experienced as very unclear for people who feel stuck, unhappy and resentful. The capacity to tolerate being the recipient of hateful and negative projections is not easily achieved; neither is the capacity to let go and accept that things cannot always be easily repaired.

Sarah, the director of a campaigning organization, told me about the challenges of her role, which required her to keep a high profile in the outside world; she said:

> One of the traps is being out there on the radio, out there in the political debate. I can occasionally send someone else, but very often they want

the director. It is good for me and I can have a lot people listening to our views. But if it is happening a lot, it can be very fragmenting. People think you are never here. There is a seductive element in being pulled outside. Sometimes it is quite difficult to make a judgement on what matters and what doesn't.

Here my biggest mistake is to promise too much and not be able to deliver. We deliver outside consistently, but inside is a different matter. I hope that magically I will be able to do everything and also temperamentally I tend to say 'yes' … It is difficult to strike the balance between letting people get on with their things and wanting to control quite a lot.

The attraction of being 'out there', knowing that it is for a useful cause as well as it being a challenging experience, can obscure the equally important need to check in, be around and available internally. The need for visibility outside the work place can become the excuse for invisibility inside it. The internal needs and the more mundane tasks can be experienced as secondary and unimportant in the context of major external challenges.

Jack, a capable manager, had developed Alton House, a day service for people with mental health problems, with passion and rigour. He had been very committed to a psychodynamic approach and had encouraged his staff to develop and train in this method. In one of our sessions together, he explained to me how the funders of the service had decided to merge Alton House with another unit that provided services for a more chronic client group who required a very different approach. Jack's world, investment and passion seemed to crumble under the fear of losing the distinctive elements he had developed over a number of years. The external threats, or perceived threats, became the enemy he had to fight. His fight became his passion – but at a cost. His capacity to be psychologically present for his staff became impaired. His staff were not equally invested in maintaining the ethos and the philosophy of Alton House: they had become more preoccupied with maintaining their jobs. Their loyalty to their manager was in conflict with their desire to reach some stability and to keep their position in the organization.

The capacity to make a distinction between one's own desires and wishes for an organization and the existence of a reality that challenges our values and way of working is a hard task. Excessive anxiety, ambition for oneself and one's organization, or political and ideological convictions, can all become major obstacles to our capacity to be fully there. Jack's situation offers a good illustration of the way in which our personality or personal 'valency' (Bion, 1961) is often unconsciously played out in the organization.

Loss of meaning and ambivalent attachment: conflict between personal ambition and organizational loyalty

In my experience, many organizations today do not seem to reward loyalty and commitment. Psychological presence requires a capacity to be available, to make space and time, and to focus on a person, a team or a situation and to put other demands on hold. It requires the capacity to be alone with a situation and experience the difficulties it brings.

Making a choice – to be loyal – is not something that people and organizations feel they can easily afford in the context of strong competition for resources and limited individual and organizational prospects. Modern technology and the increasing use of social media can speed up communication, but they can also create the illusory feeling of being connected and in touch with people without the experience of being fully engaged with a situation, an individual or a team. There is a fear of stasis, of losing opportunities if we are not in constant motion and continually 'connected' with others. Yet to be really in touch requires some 'generosity'– that unselfish feeling that parents can have towards their children – and the capacity to postpone one's own needs and desires in order to attend to other people's needs without giving up or losing sight of one's main tasks and responsibilities.

Christine, a young and committed manager of two mental health agencies, told me recently that she had had enough of her job, and could not take it anymore. She was planning to go back to agency work: she could earn more money and have more time to spend with her child. She chose to be unattached, to float in and out of organizations rather than to invest in a new and more rewarding job. This decision was the result of many factors, including personal ones. My overriding feeling was that the organization had 'failed' her. Nobody in her organization was able to tackle her disappointment, and help her to make sense of what was happening to her. Like many other organizations in the country, this one was constantly reshuffling its structure and had lost many key staff in recent years. Nobody was available to help her to move on in a constructive way.

The capacity to be psychological present in an uncertain environment requires the ability to find new meanings. Peter Marris, in his book *The Politics of Uncertainty* (1996), points out that 'We grow up, not only creating meanings, but learning to use meanings which previous generations have evolved' (p. 4). In his studies of recently widowed women, he discovered that their grief was a reaction to the disintegration of their whole structure of meaning, rather than simply a reaction to the absence of the lost person.

This concept seems very relevant to some of the dynamics of organizations today. In a context of mergers, restructuring and change, the need to mourn loss is often overlooked by management and staff (see Chapter 2 and Roberts, 2005). Organizational changes that impair our ability to make sense of our world of experience can result in a loss of meaning. Like widows, individuals and teams grieve for the loss of their structure of meaning, rather than for the loss of specific positions or situations. Yet, as Marris points out, 'however it is achieved, the recovery from a severe loss seems to depend on restoring the continuity of meaning' (p. 48). Marris goes on to remind us that grief can be all the more intense when the bereaved is deeply ambivalent towards the lost relationship.

The more unresolved the past is, the harder it is to resolve feelings about the future. In a similar way, staff, managers and teams who had an ambivalent attachment to their previous organization or organizational framework find it particularly difficult to adjust to change and to new settings. This ambivalence, often unrecognized, influences their capacity to be psychologically present in their current organization: it prevents or slows down the process of closure, adjustment to the changes and the capacity to move on. Some of the characteristics of the lost situation may be remembered in an idealized way and bad situations are not easily forgotten or forgiven.

In my view, ambivalent organizational attachment is becoming more and more a problem of our times. In the ambivalent attachment, there is an inbuilt disruptive element that can prevent any real or substantial engagement with the organization and its task. In this context, being psychologically present becomes a paradoxical task: people feel they cannot afford to be fully there. They feel only able to develop a 'loose attachment' in response to the perception that the organization is unable to respond to their needs and does not deserve their loyalty in return.

Not to be psychologically present: a malaise of our time?

The Italian sociologist Marco Brunod (2002) suggests that postmodern, post-Fordian enterprises seem to be the result, on the one hand, of an intensified quest for efficiency and productivity and, on the other hand, of a search for constant innovation and differentiation of products. He argues that there is an idealization of technological and economical factors at the expense of a marginalization of the cultural, political and value components. Short-term economic success is seen as paramount and largely informs choice. Enterprises operate in a perennial 'present', where past and future are erased, because they are perceived as obstacles to maximizing immediate results.

In this context the 'need to split', as described by Angela Foster (2001) is exacerbated: 'The paradoxical hypothesis that workers may need to split off part of their emotional experience in order to preserve their own mental health and provide reliable service to their clients' is not just an occasional psychological defence, developed in specific and particularly difficult work circumstances; it becomes a 'modus vivendi' that creates a distance between us and the world we live in. To be psychologically present in this environment is an increasing challenge. It represents a constant struggle for staff and management.

As an organizational consultant, I am constantly immersed in an environment that battles with these issues and dilemmas. Part of my work, as I see it, is to help staff and managers to 'recover a sense of meaning' (Armstrong, 1999) and to find a realistic way to engage with their task. In my work, I try to remind people that they still have choices, albeit limited ones, and that they still have some influence, even if modest.

Note

* 'The manager's most precious skill: The capacity to be "psychologically present"' was originally published in 2003 in *Organisational and Social Dynamics*, 3:3: 226–235. Reproduced by kind permission of Phoenix Publishing House.

7 Consulting to the boss
Leadership beyond the textbooks

In this chapter, I want to describe the leadership style of a number of leaders 'in practice' and to identify the key characteristics that make someone an effective leader, exploring both the benefits and the risks of their particular approach. I will focus on the concept of 'practice' as described by David Armstrong:

> ... part of the function of leadership under condition of radical uncertainty, contextual and structural, is *to make present* [my italics], through interactions with others, an idea and a feel for the 'enterprise' – or 'practice' – of the organization which can ground and recover the exchange and enactment of thought.

> ... there is a sense in which the practice may be said to frame the organization, since it is in relation to the practice and its requirements that the organization comes into being.
>
> (Armstrong, 2005, pp. 125, 132)

The leader's particular way of 'making present' represents the unique approach that shapes and inspires his or her practice, colours the experience of the organization and profoundly influences its functioning – the 'primary spirit' and 'animating principle' that give the organization 'psychic resonance' (Armstrong, 2005, p. 131).

Despite the extensive range of available courses on leadership, people mainly learn on the job, discovering what their abilities are and shaping their own unique style and approach accordingly. The way they take up their role is naturally the result of their upbringing, culture and significant work experience. Their achievements and failures are also intrinsically linked to the nature of the task, the challenges of the environment and the organizational phase at the time they are in the role.

Leadership is tough. It requires special and, at times, divergent qualities and skills. It is often a lonely position, during which leaders can be exposed to complex projections and contrasting expectations from inside and outside their organizations. In the current fluid organizational environment, with its high degree of unpredictability and uncertainty, leadership is particularly challenging. Leaders are expected to provide a containing presence in organizational environments that are not containing, with an increasing focus on performativity (see Part I).

Yet it can also provide exciting challenges and unique opportunities for implementing change and transformation. The fluidity of the environment and the technological advances could increase possibilities for innovation, entrepreneurship and new ventures if the leader is prepared to engage with a turbulent and increasingly volatile environment.

★★★

Gould talks about the concept of *holding the centre* – a reference to Yeats's poem of 1919 'The Second Coming', about the consequences of the First World War, '*Things fall apart; the centre cannot hold*' – as a core function of leadership, and the emotional challenge of '*holding the centre in the mind*' (Gould, 2010, pp. 166, 167).

The capacity to hold the centre could be connected to the idea of resilience: holding on to the essence of the organization and maintaining a sense of wholeness, even under challenging circumstances. As Gould points out, *holding on to the centre* can be linked to Melanie Klein's concept of the depressive position, in particular the capacity to tolerate ambivalence and uncertainty, an essential skill for leaders of our times (Klein, 1959).

In my consultancy experience, effective leaders all show a capacity for 'holding the centre' as well as abilities in the areas of *containment, attachment* and *taking risks* (see also Part II). They are able to contain staff's anxiety in relation to the organizational task, can form and promote meaningful attachments, and are prepared to take some risks in the service of organizational development and innovation. Depending on their different strengths and personal inclinations, they usually develop a particular capacity in one of these areas. However, it is their ability to combine elements of all these areas which makes them effective and successful leaders.

Containment

> Leadership is about interpreting anxiety … Good leadership is about helping followers to face this anxiety.
>
> (Alford, 2001, pp. 153–154)

Manuel, the head of a humanitarian organization, is a warm, paternal figure with a clear vision and a determination to succeed. His organization deals with emergency situations in the UK and abroad. Manuel knows he is good at his job, but he still feels that people outside his organization don't really understand him or get what he is trying to achieve.

He is highly respected within his own organization, though he can be experienced as quite domineering. English is his second language and his remarks are at times perceived as too direct and blunt.

Manuel has provided his team with emotional and practical containment for a long time and he has made a substantial contribution to creating a culture of care and compassion in his organization. Manuel's 'primary spirit' is the desire to create a functioning family dynamic and to encourage a sense of belonging in all his staff. In conversation he refers to his own family, sharing his feelings of affection and pride in their achievements. Similar feelings are mirrored in the way in which he relates to his team.

In leadership, being emotionally connected and using emotions as sources of thinking practice are very significant. As a consequence of Manuel's containing and emotionally tuned-in approach, his staff are quite dependent on him, particularly in times of crisis. Yet the team's powerful feeling of belonging contributes strongly to its organizational strength and its sense of sustainability into the future.

The organization reminds me of family businesses, where the emphasis is on loyalty and family values and where people from the outside are often regarded with a degree of suspicion.

Attachment

> ... the need for attachment, ... is the single most compelling motive behind the construction of meanings ... without attachments we lose our appetite for life.
>
> (Marris, 1996, p. 45)

As discussed in Part I, attachment to a meaningful activity is fundamental to our capacity to feel fulfilled and alive. The capacity to develop meaningful attachments in early life has a lasting influence (Bowlby, 1969). The capacity for attachment in a leader is an essential quality. Attachment is two-fold: it involves both the attachment to the primary task of the organization – an emotional connection and in-depth understanding of what the organization is trying to achieve – and the ability to develop meaningful relations with staff and clients.

Rachel is passionate about her work as a senior leader in a National Health Trust. She has worked in the NHS for the whole of her career and she has led a number of teams very successfully.

She is now the head of a very large service for the treatment of blood diseases. In recent years the service has expanded dramatically due to pioneering treatments and cutting-edge research. Some of the treatments have been controversial and she has faced criticism from inside and outside her organization. However, she has shown great resilience and has maintained a sense of purpose and focus throughout.

Rachel's 'primary spirit' is a strong belief in progressive medicine, and a desire to have a positive impact on the next generation. Her focus and engagement with the primary task have somehow protected her from numerous attacks by other departments inside the hospital – partly fuelled by envy of her success and her capacity to attract funding – and by external organizations, who have constantly questioned her ethics and pioneering approach. Her sense of attachment to the task in hand and her strong conviction about the overall meaning of the Trust's work have also given her a particular edge that helps her to navigate the turbulent environment of medicine and the health service.

Taking risks

> In the classic framework, risk creates anxiety, which in turn stimulates a social defence. In the framework we are considering, risk creates excitement, which stimulates by contrast, a protective frame … which in the face of danger prevents the excitement from turning into anxiety.
>
> (Hirschhorn and Horowitz, 2015, pp. 197, 210)

As Hirschhorn points out, the capacity to embrace risk and value danger can create a more rewarding connection with an environment that is turbulent and uncertain.

Alex is the founder of Flow, a successful social enterprise. The organization produces organic products and employs mainly young people, a high proportion of whom have mental and physical disabilities. He has developed Flow almost single-handedly over a number of years, with determination and passion.

Full of creative ideas and new initiatives, Alex struggles to engage with the inevitable bureaucracy of a growing organization. However, part of his success is linked to his capacity to take risks and to pioneer projects in a quite hostile environment.

His 'primary spirit' is the drive to enrich his surrounding community as well as transform much that lies beyond it, influencing current trends and attitudes to physical and mental disability.

His courage and original approach have paid off in an unstable environment where a more conventional approach would have probably failed. He can think outside the box and can move quickly from details to the bigger picture, spotting opportunities and imagining new scenarios. He is not afraid of obstacles; he can see beyond them: '… the quality of leadership is particularly relevant in situation of strategic transformation and change. A good leader has the capacity to transform strategic constrains into new challenges' (Kets De Vries, 2009, p. 2012).

The other side of the coin

The above vignettes describe success stories. These leaders have been able to engage successfully with the organizational task and have developed and transformed their organizations accordingly.

However, there have been times when even these leaders' personal valency (Bion, 1961) and their 'primary spirit' have influenced their judgement and perspectives in unhelpful ways.

Manuel, for example, had occasionally underestimated his staff's dependency on him and was surprised to learn that even senior colleagues had sometimes avoided making decisions in his absence. The 'parental containment' he provided could easily become a barrier to letting people grow and take risks, discouraging them from assuming their own authority fully.

In contrast, Rachel's passion for her task had led her to concentrate most of her energy into her clinical work and research projects. She hadn't always realized the importance of taking her team with her. Some of her staff didn't fully share her enthusiasm and had doubts about some of the service's practices and ethos. They felt they needed more guidance and attention, but she wasn't often available or around to provide this for them.

Alex had at times minimized the complexity of the environment he was in and the hostility his approach and success had generated in his community. He wasn't always prepared to deal with the mistrust and envious attacks of other organizations and political figures. He had also struggled to see the need for solid bureaucratic scaffolding for Flow. Driven by his entrepreneurial passion, he was focused on developing new ventures and new ideas, and hadn't understood the importance of creating reliable systems and processes to sustain his existing organization.

When leadership goes 'wrong'

On the problematic side, ineffective and troubled leaders lack the qualities described above and, in some cases, can be driven by *narcissistic needs, survival anxiety* or *lack of self-authorization*.

In the examples below, I illustrate how highly intelligent and skilful individuals have been unable 'to hold the centre' of their organization as a result of their anxiety, vulnerability or lack of self-authorization. Their difficulties are also linked to the dynamics and culture of their organizations, a major contributing factor to a leadership approach that could not '*make itself present*'.

A narcissistic state of mind

Tom had led Jump, a campaigning organization, from a marginal position to centre stage. In a relatively short time, he had transformed Jump into an efficient and highly regarded organization in its field.

His leadership style, which had originated in a highly competitive business background, was quite harsh and demanding. However, both the board and the senior staff had turned a blind eye to this because of Tom's abilities and the remarkable results he achieved.

When I began my involvement with Jump, the organization was going through a period of transition. Their original main objectives had been achieved and their sense of purpose was somehow diluted as a result. And, after a number of years of complete absorption in and dedication to the organization, Tom was burnt out.

In this new context, his leadership style – highly critical and quite autocratic – started to become more apparent. He was very quick to change his opinions about people and a number of individuals fell out of grace quite suddenly. Tom's 'primary spirit' was focused on creating a cutting-edge organization that projected a highly professional and competent image: he didn't forgive staff who displayed a more relaxed attitude to work and he resented criticism from inside the organization.

A leadership style that had worked during a different phase of the organization wasn't effective anymore: Tom's approach wasn't aligned with the transitional stage the organization was now going though. His staff started to feel increasingly uneasy about his approach and the board was considering taking action.

Tom represents what I would call a 'defensive narcissism', a retreat into a position of self-absorption, where his capacity for engaging productively with the external world was substantially damaged. Narcissism implies a lack of acknowledgement on our dependence on other people. Tom, with his very critical stance, seemed to disregard his need of others, possibly a defence against the anxiety of developing intimate and close relationships.

When the organization started to lose its sense of purpose, his narcissistic personality traits became more visible. His drive and quite omnipotent stance were put to good use when the organization was in a development phase. In the new phase of transition and uncertainty his approach became disconnected from the needs of the staff and the organization. He lost his capacity *to 'make himself present'*.

Survival anxiety

Monica was the head of talent in a global organization. When I first met her, I was struck by her intensity and drive. She told me she wanted to find her centre.

Despite having a young family, Monica felt dominated by her work.

She couldn't let it go or find a balance with her personal life. She was always working even when she wasn't at work: her job was always on her mind.

We connected that with her upbringing and her feelings of lack of support, particularly from her father. Now a successful senior executive, she still needed to show her ageing father how well she was doing. It was never enough.

Monica was highly regarded by her team and the CEO. This fuelled her desire to do even better. She had a compulsion to stretch herself to the limits. She was unhappy, but didn't know how to stop.

Suddenly she became very ill and had to go on sick leave for a number of months. It was at this point that she was finally able to see more clearly what she was doing and the poisonous effect of her work 'addiction' on her life.

She eventually decided to quit her job and found a less demanding position in a different firm.

While she was so hard on herself, she had a more relaxed approach towards her team, as if she was the one who had to take on the challenge of ambitious targets and the culture of 'performativity' (see Part I). Highly intelligent and perceptive, she could relate to others' people needs but struggled to acknowledge her own.

Her 'primary spirit' was creating a winning team. As the leader of talented individuals, she felt she had to role model excellence. Vulnerability and difficulties had to remain back stage. Her leadership approach was dominated by '*survival anxiety*'. Anxiety is generated by internal sources, connected to the fear of losing something 'essential to life' (Garland, 2004, p. 16).

Monica experienced herself as a survivor, someone who had done well despite her dysfunctional background. As a 'survivor' she could never relax or let go for fear of being dragged down to the unhappy place she had left behind. She chose an organization that required great stamina and drive – a fast-moving organization, with ambitious targets in a very competitive environment. The initial fit between her skills and the organizational needs gradually became a straightjacket. Rather than delegating more to her team, Monica continued to increase her input in many different projects.

When she approached me for coaching she was becoming aware that she couldn't continue to operate in this way: something needed to change. However, it was only when she got ill that she started to make some significant changes.

Lack of self-authorization

Georgina, the daughter of a successful entrepreneur, was promised the top position in her father's retail company. As the eldest of three siblings, she was seen as a potentially good leader for an expanding business. Her energy, focus on sales and toughness were seen as key ingredients for a successful CEO. Her 'primary spirit' was to develop the '*family*' business, coloured by the desire to impress her parents and family. However, her sense of entitlement and apparent confidence covered up a more complex personality, highly dependent on her father's approval and on the intervention of several external consultants.

After a number of wrong business decisions, when her father realized she wasn't as capable as he thought, he decided to sack her. The effect on Georgina was quite devastating. Her work identity was completely entangled with her family role, and her sense of competence and authority was strongly connected to her father's approval and sanction. Her 'internal' authority was weak: she couldn't see how she could achieve success and recognition outside her father's company, and felt very vulnerable.

The internalization of positive parental figures allows us to develop a sense of our own authority and value – a 'personal authority' that authorizes us from *within*. We could therefore argue that working in one's own family business doesn't allow for the necessary separation from the parents, particularly for the founders' children. In these situations, the authorization from within tends to rely on the *parent–boss* approval. The development of a separate work identity is often impaired and can create a situation of a never-ending adolescence, where there isn't clear sense of a separate identity from the original family and parents. These difficulties, emphasized in a context of family business, are also true for many people who don't feel sufficiently authorized from within and still construct a work identity on the basis of real or imagined expectations of parental figures.

The 'practice' of leadership

Generalizations about leadership are often unhelpful, as is looking for a formula or a simplified framework.

As I have described in my examples, 'making present' takes different shapes – it is often quite difficult to define and capture it. In my experience of consulting to people in leadership positions I have observed the qualities that effective leaders brought to their role and the limitations of others, who have struggled to 'hold the centre'.

Obholzer points out that authority comes from three different sources: from above, within and below (Obholzer, 2019). Leaders can't exercise their full authority if they are not sanctioned from above – by the CEO or the board – or they are not legitimized by the people they manage and lead.

Tom, with his autocratic and distant approach, lost the confidence of both the board and his senior team, while Georgina lacked the authority 'within' to inhabit a CEO role successfully.

As discussed, capacity for *containment, attachment and taking risks* are key ingredients for effective leadership in contemporary organizations.

The successful leaders I described were also able to engage with the consultancy process well. They recognized they needed some help to gain a sense of perspective on their role and on the dynamics of their organization. They could accept some dependency on me without feeling threatened or losing their sense of authority and power.

Part III

The consultant's role

An anthropologist at work

In this final part of the book, I will be examining the role and dilemmas of the organizational consultant working within the approach of the Tavistock tradition.

Part III explores the challenge of engaging with complex client systems, the risk of collusion, the dynamic of entering and ending a consultancy project, and the balance of power between consultant and client.

8   The complexity of entry

Seduction and potential collusion in negotiating a contract with a new client

Everything is there at the beginning, if we are able to see it. In Conan Doyle's story 'The Adventure of the Cardboard Box', Sherlock Holmes reflects on a successful case and reminds Watson: 'We approached the case, you remember, with an absolutely blank mind, which is always an advantage. We had formed no theories. We were simply there to observe and to draw inferences from our observations.' 'Beginnings' begin with the very first pieces of information and emotional experiences we have concerning our potential client, such as eagerness, delays, style of communications, tone of voice and body language. The physical environment and how it is used can also provide clues about key organizational dynamics (see Chapter 9). We use our *emotional intelligence* to understand what is going on below the surface: it is detective work.

As David Armstrong illustrates, emotions are not just part of our organizational experience: 'they may have something to tell us about a particular organization per se; for example the nature of its task or the way it is structured or the particular dilemmas and challenges it is facing' (Armstrong, 2005, p. 12).

Just as the ethnographer immersing him- or herself in a different culture is able to see how people live from the inside, so the consultant needs to engage with a new organization in a similar way – absorbing the organizational environment, observing its signs and symbols and trying to suspend judgement and beliefs.

Listening to the music: a feeling of displacement

Julia has taken up the offer of a few coaching sessions from her marketing firm. She sends me a brief email from her personal address, and we arrange an initial telephone conversation.

When we talk, she describes herself as a high achiever, with many qualifications and extensive experience. She is unhappy in her current role and she finds her boss difficult. Though in her fifties, people think she looks much younger. Julia grills me about my background and practice; she wants to make sure I am the right person for her. I am puzzled by her casual approach, her talking about her looks and the emphasis on her achievements. I also feel placed excessively under scrutiny about my training and career.

In our first meeting, I am impressed by how youthful and pretty Julia looks. She talks very quickly and in quite a disorganized way. She refers again to her numerous accomplishments, as if she needs to reassure herself of her worth. There is something lightweight and displaced about Julia, in spite of her efforts to convey seniority and experience. I am struck by her informal approach and her difficulty in presenting a clear picture of her organizational environment and role. She describes her boss as very ambitious and lacking in competence, while she feels unrecognized for her skills and experience.

Her account seems very one-sided.

In our next session, Julia tells me she had been forced to resign from her firm. She is angry and mortified. She says she wanted to leave and slam the door. Instead she was shown the way out before she was ready.

I am not surprised.

My initial feelings about Julia's need for reassurance and recognition seemed evidence of her precarious position in her organization. Her dismissive approach about her boss and her organization showed her ambivalent attachment towards her company and role. Writing from her personal email address conveyed a desire to keep some distance from her organization. I experienced her questioning of my credentials as a projection of her own anxiety about her competence and skills.

Julia appeared quite lost and not very transparent. She presented a picture of herself that didn't ring completely true. The initial reference to her looks was an interesting clue pointing to what emerged later: how relying on her youthful good looks had affected her career, including attracting unwanted attention and envy. Despite her training and experience, she was struggling with her sense of confidence and self-belief. She didn't know what she really wanted.

My initial experience of her and the presenting issues was key to understanding the personal and organizational dynamics at play and created the building blocks for our following work. I was able to help Julia gain some insights into how she had contributed to her difficult situation.

Harold Bridger talked of '*listening to the music* behind the words' – how we can grasp the main emotional dynamic of a song or an opera in a language we don't know. *Listening to the music* enhances our understanding of our clients' dilemmas and challenges. Tuning into the organizational music and noise is crucial to developing deeper insights into our clients' situations. The consultant's relative ignorance and naivety in engaging with a new assignment can sharpen her perception of more implicit, though significant, systemic and dynamic issues under the surface.

It is essential to hold on to our initial experience and feelings, and not to dismiss anything as irrelevant, noting what is there and also what is not there: '… Working at the edges between knowing and not knowing offers the possibility for exposure to truth-in-the moment, hence opening up the potential for learning.' (French and Simpson, 2001, p. 55).

Stranger or friend?

I always need to experience a degree of discomfort in engaging with a new individual or organizational client. I feel uncomfortable, even suspicious, when the entry into an organization is too easy. (In Chapter 10, I relate the idea of the sense of discomfort in the 'entry phase' to morning sickness at the beginning of pregnancy.) There is tension between familiarity and distance in relation to how the consultant approaches a new assignment.

Maintaining a 'stranger position' can facilitate openness – there is a seduction in talking to someone you don't know about your dilemmas and difficulties. But can we trust a stranger? The consultant can also be perceived as a disruption to the familiarity of a team or an organizational situation.

A friendly approach at the beginning can bring warmth, cooperation, but also contempt. The consultant can be seen as too familiar and, consequently, less effective and authoritative.

I was recently asked to provide some coaching to the son of a colleague. Despite the relationship with my colleague being quite distant, I was immediately experienced as somehow familiar, lacking the edge and, possibly, the authority of a complete stranger.

This sense of familiarity – of being unconsciously perceived as part of the 'extended family' – was there from the very beginning, both in the client and in myself. I was over-accommodating regarding the timings and the contract. My client was quite dismissive of my observations and suggestions from the start and often behaved in an adolescent manner, as if I were a parental figure.

Though I had a good grasp of the key issue he was facing, I didn't feel I had the complete authority to engage with him and what he was bringing to me. The consultancy stopped prematurely, possibly because of the way it was perceived from the start: as a too-familiar place.

The unwritten contract: hoping for a new birth

In a paper published many years ago, I described my first impressions when visiting Green Lodge, a residential establishment for adolescents with severe behavioural problems: 'What was immediately noticeable was how much the environment was lacking in character and the absence of children around the place. The community seemed empty and isolated....'

It was only much later that I realized the organization was facing a very uncertain future, having a low number of young residents and few new referrals. I became increasingly aware of feelings of death and impotence within the organization. This experience strongly related to how I felt in my first visit that 'its sprawling emptiness had produced in me a sense of depression' (Cardona, 1994a, p. 139, 143).

The way we engage with a potential client at the very beginning sets the scene and establishes the DNA for the project to come. Client and consultant, consciously and unconsciously, develop a *psychological contract*, which establishes the emotional context for the assignment. The *transference* to the consultant, developed in the very first contacts, influences the whole project.

My first visit to Green Lodge took place when I was pregnant. The senior staff were happy to wait until the end of my maternity leave to start the consultancy. At an unconscious level, I probably represented hope, a new birth, for an organization at risk of extinction.

Both client and consultant have unconscious expectations, desires and anxieties about the project that get often played out in the shape and format of the more formal agreement and contract (see also Chapter 10).

The number of sessions, fees structure and timing become the territory where the grit at the interface between client and consultant emerges. The practical difficulties, the delays and hiccups in engaging with the project form the background of the initial relationship and are often a sign of any ambivalence or anxiety around establishing a working alliance with the consultant.

Developing a 'good enough' working alliance with the client is essential for the life of the project – the capacity of both client and consultant to build trust in each other, without being seduced in a collusive relationship (see Chapter 10).

A family dynamic: warmth and consciousness

When I first went to see the senior team at Kelfield, a secondary school in a very deprived area, I felt immediately at home: I was welcomed, listened to and I experienced a strong affinity with the school's approach and values. The wellbeing of the children was clearly at the centre of what they were doing.

Highly aware of the challenges of their working environment, the senior team were keen to set up some reflective spaces across the whole organization, creating opportunities for staff to process the difficult situations they were facing on a daily basis.

Many years on, I am still there.

The school has developed significantly, becoming an example of good practice at a national level. Though the initial contact didn't feel particularly easy, I experienced a sense of mutual trust from the beginning. However, it took a long time to set up the consultancy, as if, after the initial positive connection, the team became more cautious and ambivalent.

Looking back, I wondered if the ambivalence and slowness in forming a working alliance with me was connected to Kelfield's organizational imprint: the school was experienced and run as a family business. As often happens in family businesses, there was cautiousness and ambivalence around welcoming 'a stranger' into the family. Could I be trusted?

The school also provides a 'surrogate family' for many children who come from very disadvantaged and dysfunctional backgrounds. The staff take great pride in their ability to hold and contain very complex young people.

The family dynamic I experienced from the start reverberated through my work with the organization over the years and remains a central component of how staff and leadership function. There is strong loyalty to the core team and to the head, who has led the organization for many years. Difficulties and incidents are dealt as much as possible internally and grievances and complaints against staff are very rare.

The family experience of my first encounter, the sense of affinity and warmth I experienced, conveyed one of the significant organizational dynamics at play. The slowness of their response to my proposal showed a different side: their fear of threat from the outside and a 'closed system' mentality.

Both initial experiences were significant in helping me to understand how the organizational system worked and what I needed to challenge.

Making links

Kay, a senior administrator at a university in a foreign country, gets in touch for a possible consultation. Our first exploratory session is on the phone: Kay sounds quite brisk and distant and she gives the impression of continuing to write on her computer while we are talking. She is under a lot pressure to implement a major reorganization project. She describes her frustration with her staff. She appears unable to delegate and seems to treat the staff as reluctant 'children'. I feel quite irritated by her lack of empathy with her team and by her distant manner with me.

When she comes to London for her first session I am surprised to meet a petite woman, quite anxious and overwhelmed by her work situation – a very different person from the formidable lady I had imagined.

> During the first session, Kay gives a picture of an incredibly stressful work environment, where she has been bullied into signing an unfair contract, which may lead to her forced resignation. The situation looks very grim and Kay is showing signs of great distress.
> I feel sorry for her and for the way she has been treated.

As soon as we end the session, I suddenly remember my first impression of her in our telephone conversation and wonder why I had forgotten it.

When we met in person, Kay wanted to address her difficult situation at work, but probably found it much easier to present only one part of herself, the 'victim persona', while keeping a more aggressive and distant part of herself 'at home'. As a consultant, I also chose to relate to the victim side as it felt more comfortable than acknowledging the initial signs of a more disruptive and ambivalent approach.

Yet making links and relating to the 'shadow' side of an organization or of an individual client is crucial for the work (Cardona and Damon, 2019). As described in the example above, it isn't just the client who wants to present a certain image of herself or her organization. The consultant too can be invested in wanting to see only one side of the story. Her own 'valency' (Bion, 1961), desires for the client and dependency on the potential work can impair her capacity to make links and bring difficult truths to the surface. The pressure from the client not to see the whole picture can be very strong and difficult to resist. (I will discuss in Chapter 10 how the 'invitation to collude' is always there, an expression of the client's unconscious wish not to change.)

The initial interaction between client and consultant can also mirror some of the dynamics of the organization: feelings of mistrust, excessive enthusiasm, passivity, desire for bonding, etc. can be 'activated' in the client–consultant relationship from the start – as highlighted in my descriptions of my first encounters with Green Lodge and Kelfield School. Paying attention to what has been projected onto us from the client can give us a taste of what it is like working in or leading that particular organization, and help us gain a sense of the main organizational dynamics and systemic issues.

How we begin

Engaging with a new assignment is a complex process, coloured by excitement and promise, but also anxiety. There is always much more to discover under the initial request and presenting issue. As I explain in Part II, there is a *red thread* that starts to emerge at the beginning, representing the core issue and anxiety of the client: the sense of something lightweight and displaced about Julia, the feelings of death and impotence about Green Lodge, the familiar and cautious response of Kelfield School were all there at the start. However, in these instances, I couldn't fully identify and understand my initial reactions. It took some time to be able to make relevant connections between my feelings and the organizational dynamics.

Identifying and connecting the evidence together is a sophisticated craft, which requires a capacity to stay with what has been presented, immersing oneself in the client's environment and accepting the mess, uncertainty and sense of overwhelm the process often entails. It means starting where the client is.

A lot happens at the interface in the initial negotiation phase: the consultant begins to form an understanding and assessment of the client's situation, while the client starts to develop a transference relationship to the consultant and to the project. The foundation of the relationship between client and consultant happens in this zone, forming the DNA of the project. The *psychological contract* develops in parallel to the formal contract, providing the emotional texture. Some of the process remains unconscious or in the 'unthought known' area (Bollas, 1987) and might come to the surface at a later stage.

The interest and curiosity of the consultant and the client's capacity to be open are essential ingredients in this initial stage.

While beginnings can be very different, depending on the organizational task, the nature of the client's issue and the overall context – the *dynamic of entry* with its expectations, doubts, ambivalence and desire – is a common denominator to all.

9   The consultancy stage

The 'third' dimension in the engagement between client and consultant

Physical spaces have a powerful role in enhancing, inhibiting and developing psychological work, and can strongly influence the consultancy engagement. By observing how individuals and teams use, relate to and engage with different spaces, it is possible to understand some of the underlying organizational and leadership dynamics. The choice of location, space, furniture and colour can convey key elements of the organizational culture and task, which in turn helps us to understand the wider context in which the work takes place.

The consultant's experience of working in different settings can also influence her creativity and capacity to think: 'A building is not an end to itself; it frames, articulates, restructures, gives significance, relates, separates and unites, facilitates and prohibits. Consequently, elements of an architectural experience seem to have a verb form rather than being nouns' (Pallasmaa, 1994).

Through a number of vignettes, I am going to consider what is projected onto the physical space where work takes place, its objects and ambience, and to discuss how the 'stage' represents the 'third party' in the relationship between client and consultant.

A modern open space: identity and secrecy

Claire, the leader of a successful policy think tank, Melt, has often referred to the open-plan arrangement of their office as a sign of her organization's transparency and non-hierarchical structure. She doesn't have her own office, despite her high profile inside and outside the organization.

We usually meet in a meeting room with glass walls near the reception desk. This time she looks very upset. 'I have major issues with my deputy', she whispers. I sit in my usual position, with my back to the door. After a couple of minutes she asks me to swap seats. She is concerned that her staff might 'lip-read' or understand what we are discussing.

Later on in the consultation, I link this incident with an organization that wants to present itself as modern and open minded – the contemporary building, open-plan design and glass walls – but which struggles with an underlying culture of secrets, gossip and at times unprofessional relationships.

Melt's staff were proud of their contemporary and open approach, which was reflected in their choice of building and layout – with no dedicated space for the director. The leadership team often emphasized their difference from the public sector with respect to their effectiveness, lack of traditional hierarchy and clear focus. They were rightly proud of their many significant achievements in their sector.

In my individual sessions with Claire, I heard how the organization had a history of a lack of boundaries, including sexual relationships among staff, and a gossip culture. She believed she had introduced a more professional and bounded culture. However, she behaved with me in quite an unbounded way, sharing a lot of personal details about her staff in a 'gossipy' manner and regularly targeting different members of the leadership team as incompetent and unable to meet her expectations. This often left me uneasy. Despite my numerous attempts, Claire resisted addressing some of the issues she raised with me in the meetings with her leadership team. The open-plan arrangement of the office was a paradoxical representation of what was going on among the staff. The physical environment looked open and transparent, but the reality was an organization struggling to show society what it really was.

The nature of the task – to provide policies and advise in the field of minority rights – appeared to have created two 'parallel' worlds: a 'public' world which represented how they wanted to be seen – as a modern, professional and open-minded organization; and another world – a closed system that didn't trust 'the other' and the establishment. There was a subtle but pervasive sense of grievance towards the establishment at the core of the organization, a widespread suspicion about mainstream society and a culture of secrecy. Many of Melt's employees came from minority groups and many of them had personal experience of marginalization.

I tried to model a different way of communicating, where relevant information and experiences were openly discussed and didn't remain implicit, but I experienced a constant challenge to this approach right to the end of my intervention. In my meetings with the leadership team, I felt a strong pressure to avoid making links with themes and concerns discussed in my individual sessions with the director. There was a pressure to keep the difficult stuff hidden under the carpet and to maintain a cool and efficient appearance where mess and differences had very little space. In this way, the 'bad parts' would firmly belong elsewhere and the director's scapegoat approach remained unchallenged.

This dynamic seemed related to a complex organizational identity and a fear of exclusion connected to the staff's and the stakeholders' personal history of marginalization. The open-plan environment and flat hierarchy provided a façade behind which they could hide and attempt to protect themselves from anxiety about their identity and uncertainty about entitlement. You could argue that the modernity and open-plan layout of the physical environment represented an aspiration to cutting-edge professionalism and lack of differentiation in order to counterbalance or defy the sense of exclusion that was still very much alive in the organization and amongst its members.

A grand old house: attachment to space and the difficulty of being 'ordinary'

When I entered this building I always felt a sense of history and tradition; there was something special and unique that enveloped you. The house, located in a small village in the countryside, had handsome features and a beautiful extensive garden. Yet the building itself looked quite tired and in need of refurbishment. It had been left by a benefactor to Vine, a private organization for disturbed young people.

Vine had successfully pioneered innovative treatments and had established a high reputation in its field, both at home and internationally. In recent years, it had struggled to raise enough funding and it was now catering for a much smaller number of patients. Moreover, its role in the field of mental health was now less relevant, due to a more general shift in the mental health sector to short-term and more affordable treatments. However, the staff still took great pride in their way of working and felt they provided a unique service. Vine's in-depth and well-developed treatment programme had helped generations of young people and produced significant results.

In recent times, there have been talks of selling the property to help fund the organization, and moving to a less prestigious building. The team has struggled to consider this plan as a viable option. Vine's reputation and image are strongly linked to the beautiful old building: the branding of the organization is very much connected to where the organization 'lives'. Staff argue that patients have a strong transference towards the building, which they believe has a reparative function for people with years of emotional and physical deprivation.

Implications for staff and leadership

Vine's *organizational stage* provides a sense of continuity, history and a feeling of being special. Just as an impoverished aristocratic family might struggle to acknowledge their change of status and circumstances, so Vine's leadership and staff have an entrenched reluctance to separate their professional identity and status from the building. There are of course very legitimate reasons for hanging on to the house: the countryside location and the beauty and generosity of the space have provided patients with a therapeutic environment very hard to match. For many patients, the physical environment has been a strong influence on their wellbeing and recovery process. On the other hand, it has also represented a sense of being special and different that has diminished the staff's capacity to look outward and engage more proactively with the community.

As a consultant, I have had to resist the invitation to join in the feeling of being 'special'. One of my main objectives, while acknowledging the tradition and the good practice, has been to foster a capacity of being 'ordinary' and to encourage the leadership to open up, practically and meta-phorically, the building to the wider environment.

Vine's organizational stage has been both an asset and a hindrance that has coloured the development of the organization. Making staff and leadership more aware of the defensive element in their relatedness to the building has helped to create new ways of engaging with the broader context. The appointment of new senior staff has injected new energy and ideas about the use and layout of the building. People have started to develop plans for invit-ing members of the community in: hosting local projects and reorganizing the available space to make it more open and user-friendly. However, despite these efforts, it has taken a long time to develop any new initiative. Somehow the DNA of the building, its history and the well-established practice can't be shifted – as if there were an unconscious anxiety that any substantial change to the building would threaten the identity of the organization and con-sequently the staff's own identity.

The 'attachment to place' – 'the bonds that individuals develop with places over time – a sense of connection built up gradually as individuals occupy, use and experience a given environment' (Manzo and Devine-Wright, 2014, p. 80) – is a significant lens through which to perceive the emotional dynamics of the work place. As Pallasmaa suggests, we are in constant dia-logue and interaction with the environment, to the point where it can become impossible to detach the image of self from its spatial existence (Pallasmaa, 1994).

Waiting at the threshold – crossing from the outside to inside

During the consultancy with a family business, I was struck by how long it took me to be allowed into the company's building. It was only at the very end of the intervention that I and my colleagues were invited into their work space, an interesting period building, full of memorabilia relating to the com-pany's history and successes. Before this, our meetings with the family had taken place in the aseptic environment of hotel boardrooms. There was a sense that we were kept waiting at the entrance until they could finally trust us enough to be allowed into their 'home'.

Our intervention was coloured by ambivalence from the beginning.

The focus of the intervention, which involved the transition of leadership from the first to the second generation, was complex. The family had experi-enced many difficulties and conflicts among themselves both in their personal and business roles. There was a lack of trust between the siblings and doubts about their capacity to work together effectively. So it wasn't surprising that they felt ambivalent towards us, 'the outsiders', and kept us waiting. This atti-tude was emphasized by the fact they were a 'family' business. Despite all their difficulties, they were still a 'family' who wanted to keep 'outsiders' out to protect and possibly hide what was within. In the last session we were finally invited into their company and shown around the building. There was more trust, but also the realization that we were on our way out.

Family systems are usually closed units that are often suspicious about people outside the family. All through this project, we had to deal with our clients' ambivalence and lack of trust. It mirrored their lack of trust in each other and in their parents. The whole intervention was coloured by a fear of becoming dependent on us because of their difficult experience of being dependent on their parents (Cardona and Raffaelli, 2016).

Having been allowed 'into' their work home coincided with a moment of significant growth for this group on both systems, family and business. They seemed more able to trust us and share with us their organizational space and, more concretely, symbols of their business achievements.

My own stage – my consulting room: containment, competition, familiarity and ambivalence

I see a number of coaching clients in my consulting room, a self-contained part of my house. People engage with the space in different ways. Some people comment on the room and the neighbourhood; others use it in a very functional way, showing no interest in the physical context. Their response to the environment often seems connected to the issues and dilemmas that they bring with them, in relation to where they are in their personal life and work.

Laura, a senior nurse leader, has done very well, despite her modest background. She had a very dynamic and successful career and she is considering her 'last act' before retirement. I wonder if her remarks and curiosity about my neighbourhood suggest that she thinks I have done better than her. Always very focused and quite concrete in her thinking, she struggles to bring her more vulnerable side to the sessions. She wants to appear confident and on top of things. I find it challenging to encourage her to explore grey areas and address her doubts about her role, knowing she could interpret this as implying that she hasn't done as well as she thinks she has.

On the other hand, Javier, a young and ambitious banker, loves my consulting room. He often comments on the paintings on the walls and says he feels calm and relaxed when he is there. He comes from a close and well-off Spanish family who have encouraged him to move to London. He feels the pressure to succeed, but also misses his family very much. He has come to me through a colleague, who is a friend of his family. The 'family' connection emphasizes his wish for a familiar environment where he can bring his doubts and be himself. The finance world is tough and demanding and he often feels overwhelmed. He doesn't really know what he wants. During our sessions, he moves from planning a conventional career in finance to talking about new ventures in very different fields.

In another consulting room where I work, Moira, a highly stressed leader of a large NHS service, sips with pleasure the cup of tea brought by our secretary. 'This is the best bit', she often says. For someone who has little time for herself and who has a very demanding and stressful job, sitting in this small room with a cup of tea is a 'treat'. This modest and quite unattractive room becomes a refuge from the bombardment of emails and the relentless demands from her staff and patients.

The virtual stage of Skype: emotional engagement in the virtual stage

Fiona sent me a message just an hour before her session, saying she wasn't feeling very well. 'Could we Skype?' she asked.

I felt quite annoyed by the short notice, but I accepted. I never looked forward to our sessions. She worked in finance and seemed quite rigid and concrete in her approach. It was hard work encouraging her to think more laterally and address issues under the surface.

On my computer screen Fiona looked distressed. She didn't have her usual immaculate appearance and was close to tears. She described an upsetting incident with her boss and she gradually started to relax. She could see that the situation wasn't so bad and we started to look at possible ways of dealing with it. At one point I saw her moving and looking down: suddenly a little dog appeared on the screen. She had been holding it on her lap all the time; it clearly provided comfort and a feeling of safety.

I was struck afterwards how the Skype session had allowed Fiona to work from her own home, and how, for the first time, she was able to engage more fully with the session, allowing her emotions to surface. Perhaps the 'screen' also offered a degree of distance, a defence that allowed her to open up more freely.

I had a similar experience with Jo, the wife of a senior executive, who was based in an African country. She wanted some help to set up her own business. It wasn't easy. She had a young family, her husband's career was very demanding and the systems of the African country were complex and unhelpful. We had met a couple of times in London and then we arranged a Skype session.

She looked at ease and relaxed in her own environment, despite the difficulties she had described about her situation. I could see a room with a lot of light pouring through the windows and some interesting pictures on the wall. Differently from our conversations in London, Jo seemed more positive about her situation and clearer about the steps she needed to take. It was as if the 'marriage' between the coaching session and her world was more productive in the virtual setting.

More and more people are using virtual settings for coaching and consultancy meetings. Geographical distance and the pressures of modern life make them essential spaces for these activities. At some level the virtual setting is more demanding: the connection is rarely smooth and it requires concentration and discipline. I have always regarded it as second best to face-to-face meetings.

Krantz, in his paper on 'Social defences in the information age', wonders if virtualization provides an easy avenue for avoiding meaningful relationships and authentic experience, and if the illusion of proximity in time and space distorts our connection to the world (Krantz, 2015, p. 67). However, my experience with Fiona and Jo makes me think differently about virtual consultancy. In both their situations, it provided a more effective 'consultancy stage'. Both clients were able to feel grounded in their familiar territory. From that 'safe' base, they were able to engage differently with me and overcome some of the barriers of a more conventional space where they felt less connected. Skype is quite a leveller, a more democratic way of engaging in the consulting exchange. The potential disadvantages of the virtual element and the physical distance are balanced by the connection with a familiar base that might create more possibilities.

The consultancy stage as a third dimension – 'inside and outside can only exist together'

My thinking about consultancy stages is very much influenced by Winnicott's ideas about transitional spaces and holding environments, and by Bion's concepts of 'container' and 'contained'. The central idea is that physical space and what is projected into it are very significant for holding and understanding the client's organizational and emotional dynamics.

Bion's theory of container and contained argues that 'the relations between the two are reciprocal, the container influencing the contained, and the contained influencing the container' (Armstrong and Rustin, 2015, p. 5). Winnicott talks about how the baby cannot exist separately from the relationship with the holding environment. There is an interactive dynamic between the environment and those individuals who inhabit it.

Work activities and work interactions happen in places, and these places are permeated by our own emotions and meanings. They also 'provide experiences in their own right': the smell of damp, the brightness of the colours, the paintings on the walls, etc. (Izod, 2016, p. 117). Organizations and leaders choose particular buildings and engage with them in their own way, projecting in their engagement with the physical space some of the key dynamics at the core of their task and role. Physical space also gives an idea of how organizations and staff see themselves – their 'organization in the mind' (Armstrong, 2005). Meeting in a physical space provides a third party – a context to the conversation.

There is a difference between 'the geometrical space (measurable by the natural science and mathematics) and the *anthropological space* immeasurable and unthinkable but "emotionally attuned"' (Schinaia, 2016, p. 41).

I am referring here to the anthropological space that contains a number of physical and emotional factors contributing to the understanding of and the engagement with the organizational reality.

And then there is an interaction between the people who inhabit a space and the space itself. The architect Daniel Libeskind says:

the physical space is good for physicists. It is not the architectonical space
... although it is made of glass and bricks, a building is constituted by
something else. It is the invisible! ... this invisibility certainly comes from
the function and the aim of the place, but implies also something broader
moving me as a fundamental perceptive experience. It is the character of
the architecture of the room ... that sensation connecting the room with
my internal activity, with those peculiar sensations that are more
meaningful.

(Schinaia, p. 52)

Being aware of the impact and significance of the physical environment in
the consultancy engagement can help to develop a *transitional* space that can
be containing, challenging and transforming.

10 Who is the boss?*

Balancing power and vulnerability in the client–consultant relationship

They that have power to hurt and will do none.

(Shakespeare, Sonnet 94)

I meet with Annabel, the director of a very successful company, to discuss some possible consultation to her organization. The atmosphere is friendly, though quite cautious. We both know one of the main reasons we are meeting is her recent breakdown. She has been on sick leave for a number of weeks and has reluctantly accepted the need to invest in, and delegate more to, her senior team. Annabel is a formidable and extremely competent leader, who has developed her organization significantly. Her breakdown has signalled to her and to the rest of the organization that something has to change, in particular her centralized approach. The breakdown is not a secret, but it is something almost unspeakable. I have to force myself to mention it as an important factor in our preliminary discussion. I am also aware that this potential assignment could be a substantial and very interesting project: it would give me the opportunity to work in a new field and with an organization facing exciting challenges.

This brief vignette illustrates the main focus of this chapter: the dynamic of power and vulnerability between client and consultant.

Is it Annabel who is in a position of vulnerability in relation to the consultant? She had a breakdown and needs help to change and develop her leadership approach.

Or is the consultant (myself) the vulnerable one? I am eager to be involved with the organization and depend on Annabel's experience of me to secure this assignment.

In this chapter the dynamic of power and vulnerability are linked to issues of trust, interdependence and the risk of collusion. Through a number of examples I intend to address the complexity of the relationship between client and organizational consultant and the need for constant adjustment, mutual challenge and review.

The risk to trust

Trust is a fundamental element in the relationship between client and consultant. When there is ambivalence in their trust in one another, the fragile balance of power and vulnerability can collapse and give way to disruptive dynamics that can have a damaging effect well beyond the scope of the project.

Trust is not a given. To accept someone else's help requires trust not just in the other, but also in oneself. As Sievers points out:

> Many authors rightly emphasize that trust not only manages risk, uncertainty and expectations, but also requires 'one party's willingness to be vulnerable to another party' … The greater the risk trust has to 'absorb', the greater the capacity required to cope with the loss when one's trust is violated.
>
> (Sievers, 2009, p. 231)

Trust cannot be engineered: it is a fluid process that needs regular confirmation and reviewing. At the beginning of any assignment both client and consultant take a risk. I have argued earlier that there is a need to experience some degree of discomfort when we engage as consultants with a new organization. I compare this idea to the morning sickness in the first phase of pregnancy, a phase of adjustment between the body of the mother and the foetus.

Ambivalence, anxiety and suspension of trust are important ingredients in the engagement and developmental stages of a shared project. An initial ambivalence could be a useful antidote to mutual idealization, excessive expectations and collusion. A client (individual, or organizational) might protect himself from trusting the consultant as a defence against shame – the shame of needing help, being seen as vulnerable, incompetent or ineffective. As mentioned at the start of Chapter 3, Hunt has argued that:

> Shame … represents the affective experience of the sense of inadequacy of the self, of not being up to the task or of being defective … The individual experiences shame in response to a sense that he 'is' a failure, not that he 'has' failed.
>
> (Hunt, 2000)

On the other hand, a consultant might maintain an ambivalent relationship with the client for fear of being seen in financial need, in a dependency position or in search of professional recognition. The decision to risk trusting means accepting the dependency on the other and the reciprocity this entails.

Annabel did give me the job and I am now consulting to her organization. She has developed some trust in me, just… a popular and successful leader, Annabel constantly struggles to give me the authority and the power to intervene in her organization. After all, who am I to point out deficiencies in the organization's approach, lack of proper delegation or excessive criticism of their competitors?

I often feel on my guard when I venture some hypotheses or comment on how they work together. As during my initial interview, I sense that I need to be cautious about what I say and how I say it. The power balance is particularly relevant in an organization that has developed from a fringe position and is now perceived as more mainstream and influential. The original imprint is of an organization at the 'margins', and this psychological 'position' re-emerges regularly when the organization feels criticized or is under stress.

The power to intervene and the power to hire

A couple of years ago I was invited to negotiate a potential piece of work with a very well-known organization in the arts field. The assignment was very small, but the significance for me of being involved with that organization was incredibly high. I vividly remember the feeling of elation after the first meeting: I felt I had finally 'made it'; I was working with one of the finest British institutions.

On the one hand I had a genuine anthropological interest in discovering a new organizational world and understanding what was going on under the surface, on the other hand I had a fantasy that I could have a real impact on such a prestigious organization.

The hope of 'a lucky break' is a constant element in the artist's engagement with work: painters, dancers, actors and musicians all wait for 'that' special moment when, from obscurity, they will become widely appreciated and well known. Feeling so elated and excited, I was mirroring an experience very common among artists from all disciplines. I was also experiencing a moment of potential power or potency when I was given the opportunity to make a difference, unlock a difficult situation, address a conflict and introduce some changes.

Power is a loaded concept. It constrains us, but it also makes things possible. Without some degree of power we cannot make any effective intervention: 'authority, though necessary, is not sufficient' (Obholzer, 2001, p. 201). The consultant's power provokes anxiety not only in the client, but also in the consultant. Experiencing the expectations and vulnerability of the client can be challenging, as well as the realization of one's own power and capacity to influence. Knowing that something significant could be developed and being an instrument for substantial and meaningful change can be exhilarating.

The first meeting with a client is often full of promises: the desire, both conscious and unconscious, to create a productive partnership as well as the anxiety of having a sterile encounter are present and in the room alongside the conversation. The exhilaration and dread in the client and in the consultant originate from leaving familiar places and embracing new possibilities.

It is at this point of the engagement that both consultant and client are most vulnerable. I often find myself with the desire to impress: to show my skills, wisdom and insights. I can also feel quite deskilled and uncertain, as if I had suddenly lost my capacity to understand, assess and intervene effectively. The client might feel very mixed towards this new experience, feeling in need of some help and understanding, being both excited and anxious about the prospect of changes and developments, fearing to show his vulnerability, concerns and difficulties.

The possibility of change can evoke strong primitive anxieties: the fear of pulling apart something familiar, well established and containing. Krantz states:

> Effective change requires sophisticated effort ... Yet it is the very features of organizational life that protect them from intrusion of primitive pro-
> cesses − its social defence system − that are at the same time being dis-
> mantled ... Consequently, efforts to innovate confront organizations with a paradox of change: change undermines features of organizational life that foster the very qualities of functioning required to make change succeed.
>
> (Krantz, 2001, p. 136)

In this 'paradoxical' context the consultant might also feel the pressure not to challenge the status quo and he can unconsciously collude with the client's wish not to change.

In a paper I co-wrote with Wendy Bolton we explored what we have called 'the invitation to collude'. When a client (individual, team or organiza-
tion) is in a process of change or experiencing problems, it is likely that a consultant may be experienced as potentially threatening as well as potentially helpful. A consultant is called in when a client decides that they need 'outside' help − something different from inside − but it is the differentness of the consultant which the client attempts to eliminate for fear of what she might see or for fear of her criticism.

Anne Marie Sandler argues that the stage of stranger-anxiety − when the child of around eight months is frightened by the appearance of a stranger is distinct from fearing the loss of one's mother − is about the experience of disruption of the dialogue with the mother by the intrusion of the 'markedly unfamiliar', the dissonance of the strange (Sandler, 1977).

The consultant's own needs may also come into play. He may be more prone to fitting in with what a client wants him to be, seeing things from their point of view and losing his difference, if he feels under pressure from his own needs. This can add to the likelihood of complying with the invitation to collude. The consultant can be experienced by members of the group as threatening the cohesion either by proposing changes or by drawing atten-
tion to the vulnerability and conflicts within the group. When the organiza-
tion is feeling vulnerable, the consultant may be experienced as the stranger threatening disruption (Bolton and Cardona, 2004).

The client can also exercise a substantial degree of power by hiring a consultant. 'The power to hire' can have a significant impact on the relationship

if the consultant feels too dependent on the assignment to be able to challenge the client or to quit if he feels ineffective.

As consultants we should be open to be fired at any stage. This is not easily achieved. The capacity to review our role and effectiveness is often contaminated by our desire to influence and by our need to work.

The vulnerability of asking for help brings with it the potential for negative transference. Vulnerability comes from the Latin *vulnus*, which means wound.

★★★

The director of a therapy centre for young people realized his staff needed some help to address the complexity and challenges of their work. A very sophisticated group, they were however quite ambivalent about accepting consultancy input. They were used to being the 'helpers' and found the process of showing their own difficulties and vulnerabilities painful. The director was particularly defensive in his approach. He regularly corrected and edited my hypotheses and seemed to struggle every time I commented on an area of difficulty. Paradoxically, having been 'soaked' in other people pain and difficulties made the staff more resistant to look at their own pain, conflicts and differences. Having to show real vulnerability to each other and to me was like reopening a 'wound'.

The staff of the therapy centre struggled to allow me to 'see' their individual and organizational vulnerabilities. They treated me at times just as a 'convener' of the group with very little influence and not much to contribute. The feeling of shame and the fear of dependency translated into an ambivalent transference towards me.

As a consultant I knew I had both to absorb and challenge their response. Engaging with and recognizing their negativity was an important step towards creating a more balanced relationship where accepting their dependency needs did not mean they were becoming powerless.

The anxiety of showing one's own vulnerabilities, as well as the fear of becoming dependent on the consultancy input, colours the relationship and the transference towards the consultant. Tim Dartington makes a distinction between primitive and mature dependency: 'In its primitive sense dependency derives from a frightening and frightened state of mind, where the immature organism looks desperately in its environment for a reliable object to save it from an unimaginable danger' (Dartington, 2010, p. 42).

A mature dependency, in contrast, starts from a sociometric perspective, where, in the words of John Donne, 'No man is an island, entire of itself'. It is an interactive process that requires 'both thought and action, where there is recognition of difference and a use of difference to achieve mutually agreed ends' (p. 44).

Dartington points out that the distinction between primitive and mature dependency is not always clear-cut. It is the fear of the 'primitive' dependency that is often behind a negative transference or profound ambivalence. Melanie Klein talks about the importance of the integration between positive and negative transference, and links this to the early interplay between love and hate: 'The analysis of the negative as well as of the positive transference and their interconnection is … an indispensable principle for the treatment of all types of patients' (Klein, 1975, p. 53). 'Because life and death instincts and therefore love and hatred are at the bottom in the closest interaction, negative and positive transference are basically interlinked' (p. 54).

Later, when discussing the process of integration during analysis, Klein emphasizes the importance of establishing the patient's capacity for love: '… one should not underrate the loving impulses when these can be detected in the material. For it is these which in the end enable the patient to mitigate his hate and envy' (p. 226). There may be a tendency to focus on interpreting aggression and to avoid the interpretation of loving feelings because of the fear of giving reassurance. But Klein clearly states that love and hate need to be brought together because interpretation of a patient's split-off hatred without an acknowledgement of loving feelings that will mitigate the hatred tends to result in persecutory anxiety rather than integration (Halton, 2011).

In organizational consultancy, the positive transference has a more explicit and central place between client and consultant. There isn't too much space for regression in a consultancy setting. However, like the Gestalt concept of the figure/ground relationship, the negative transference doesn't disappear. Sometimes in the consultancy process the negative transfer has to move from ground to figure to allow more explicit work on negative and disruptive dynamics. Dealing with negative transference can be challenging for client and consultant, as they can both resist the need to address negative and disruptive feelings in their relationship and can highlight vulnerability both in the client and in the consultant. 'Living with vulnerability means accepting and understanding one's limitations and yet continuing to live in an area that is unsafe' (Dartington, 2010, p. 116).

Creating a shared context

Music is the silence between the notes.

(Debussy)

The creation of a shared context of understanding and collaboration between client and consultant builds a base that allows the dynamics of power and vulnerability to be addressed and managed.

Winnicott talks of 'potential space': 'an intermediate area between subjectivity and objectivity, between fantasy and reality, an area of illusion and compromise' (Amado, 2009, p. 264). As Amado points out, organizations might feel threatened by potential spaces because they bring with them ambiguity, doubts and ambivalence.

Building a 'shared context' or a 'third space' is an essential element of the consultancy journey. This third space can exist if there is a common understanding and shared sense of the emotional meaning of the organizational purpose.

Halton talks of the 'evolutionary creativity' triggered by the need to develop, which is connected to a capacity for openness to uncertainty: 'It is based on the need for further development within the depressive position' (Halton, 2004, p. 111). It requires a mental attitude of patience. 'The transition from an old synthesis to a new one involves a period of flux during which there are feelings of loss and gain' (p. 112). '… the emotional components are: depression, elation and anxiety. Depression because something is lost, elation because something new is coming, and anxiety because the future is unbounded and uncontained' (p. 116).

We could look at the consultancy relationship as an expression of evolutionary creativity where the power of co-creating something new is mixed with the anxiety of facing individual, group and organizational vulnerabilities.

The challenge for the consultant is to regulate the 'distance' from the client in providing a setting that is both intimate and sufficiently distant to allow for new thinking to take place, creating a context where clients can allow the consultant to see their vulnerabilities without feeling disempowered. Paradoxically, creativity requires both togetherness and separation.

Evolutionary creativity can 'give rise not only to hope, but also to envy. This envy is based on the feeling that the new idea was conceived by someone else … and not by oneself. Envy of creativity intensifies resistance to change' (Halton, p. 118). Envy, and fear of envy, need to be managed and recognized as key ingredients of the consultancy process.

Consultants should also be open to challenging their own dependency from the clients and be aware of the risk of being 'invited' to collude. The experience of being needed, of representing a positive and powerful figure, could prevent the consultant from maintaining a critical edge and letting go when it is time to end the assignment.

Ending should be considered from the outset and should always be kept in view to underline the transitional nature of the consultancy intervention. It is important to accept the transient nature of our work by leaving some of our work unfinished and giving up our omnipotent feelings.

Note

* 'Who is the boss? Balancing power and vulnerability in the client- consultant relationship' has been published in H. Brunning, *Power and vulnerability*, London: Karnac, 2014.

11 Ending and regeneration
Reflections on the emotional experience of ending a consultancy assignment

Endings are never easy: they provoke primitive feelings of death and finality, of being got rid of or disposed of. As in life, organizational endings can be premature, murderous or well prepared. Endings can also represent a beginning, regeneration or a new stage in the existence of an organization.

How might the process of ending play out in consultancy arrangements? What is the emotional significance of closing a contract and terminating a relationship?

The way a team, department or organization ends its consultancy can also be very revealing of how the organization manages its own significant endings and how prepared it is to enter a new stage or phase of its development. It can, moreover, be a learning experience enabling the client to handle other endings differently, and as such can usefully be regarded as an integral stage of the consultancy project.

In the current environment of constant change and transition, of reshuffles and mergers, endings have become a constant feature of organizational life. Yet endings are frequently overlooked and their effect on workers and on organizational structures are often underestimated or played down. Today, endings are especially difficult because of the uncertainty of postmodern organizations: when we leave an organization we do not know what will happen to it, and if it will be there in a few years' time.

Ending and organizational grief

The major difficulty about endings is connected with anxieties about loss. These anxieties can be equally true for both client and consultant. Individuals, teams and organizations have to go through a process of mourning, of giving up previous situations, to be able to move on to a new context.

The loss must be recognized if we wish to integrate the important elements of what is not there anymore. Grieving represents the conflict between the wish to maintain the lost relationships and situations, and the need to get rid of the painful feelings connected to the loss; wanting to maintain the significant elements of the past while wishing to create something different and new. In grief and in significant transitions there is no possibility of going back: individuals, groups and organizations need to re-organize themselves:

> According to Peter Marris new experiences can be assimilated when they are placed in the context of a familiar, reliable construction of reality. Resistance to change is not only protection of the old and rejection of the new but a holding on to a secure reference point from which is possible consider adapting to the new.
>
> (Hughes and Pengelly, 1997, p. 135; Marris, 1993)

The 'capacity to end' is related to our capacity to accept the limits of our intervention and to leave space for others to continue the work if necessary. It is linked to the ability to deal with our own desires to be thought of as essential, indispensable, and to our narcissistic tendencies: the wish, conscious and unconscious to be wanted, appreciated and unique; it relates to the capacity of giving up ideas about perfection or of exerting total control over a situation.

Dependency is an inevitable part of a consultant's role. The difficulty is, as Eric Miller points out, how to respond to dependency needs without creating a dependent organization The attraction of having people dependent on you is strong: it gives an imaginary power and certainty to the role of the organizational consultant, which is a relatively new professional role 'on the boundary between craft and profession' (Miller, 1993).

Ending any situation is also a reminder of a more definitive end, and of our fears of death and annihilation. Elliot Jaques in his paper on 'Death and the middle-life crisis' (1965) argues that in early adulthood people tend to deny and defend themselves against the inevitability of eventual death, and the existence of hate and disruptive impulses inside oneself: 'The explicit recognition of these two features and the bringing them into focus, is the quintessence of successful weathering of the mid-life crisis and the achievement of mature adulthood' (Jaques, 1965, p. 505). In a similar way 'mature' organizations should be able to recognize and acknowledge the relevance of their own endings.

Whatever the level, the depth and the nature of the engagement of our intervention, we are inevitably involved in some of the processes and dynamics described above.

Our capacity as consultants to recognize organizational processes, to help our clients to engage with complex dynamics and to do something about their situation makes our work worthwhile. When this process gets interrupted it can be painful and difficult to bear. We can feel rejected and unappreciated or not good enough for the assignment. Or we might worry about the client organization, about its capacity to work without a proper support system.

The client organization might experience contradictory impulses: the wish to assert their independence and maturity mixed with the fear of being abandoned and left behind. When these feelings are not acknowledged and worked through, the organization might act in a more radical and abrupt way in the attempt to cut off or cover up its dependency needs and feelings of loss.

This dynamic mirrors one of the central processes of adolescence: when are the parents ready to let the young person go, leave home, and when is the young person ready to leave? Is it the parents who have to throw the adolescent out or is it the adolescent who has to slam the door?

It is also a question of power: who is the person who makes the final decision about who is leaving and who is being left behind?

As I have argued in a previous chapter, the consultant's power provokes anxiety not only in the client, but also in the consultant. Experiencing the expectations and vulnerability of the client can be challenging, as well as the realization of one's own power and capacity to influence.

As consultants, we may have to give up a piece of work that gives us pleasure, validation and income. I remember announcing to a team with whom I have being working for many years my intention to end the consultancy. I had experienced the tiredness and lack of motivation of the staff for many months and tried to address it without much success. The first reaction to my announcement was: 'You have not consulted us', as if I could not take a unilateral decision. They felt robbed of their 'ending power'.

Harold Bridger, in his lecture on groups, referred to the concept of '*mutual rejection*' involved in the birth process, when the mother and the foetus reach a point when they both have enough and need to move on to a new stage. Both have to relinquish previous situations of satisfaction if they are to develop. This idea seems very relevant to the concept of ending. 'In 'Mourning and Melancholia' (1917) Freud linked the preservation of sanity and reality to the relinquishment of the idea of the permanent possession of the love object' (Britton, 1992, p. 39). The capacity to mourn is key to the capacity to regenerate and move to a different stage.

The acceptance of death, losses and transitions can give us a sense of meaning. 'In Bion's view the very capacity to think develops from the infant experience of absence of "no-thing" which, well enough contained, can become a thought' (French and Simpson, 2001). Being able to separate and end can give space to develop an internal capacity to consult, in the individual and in the organization. However, shifts and constructive outcomes are frequently not immediately visible. It might take time to realize that things have changed or can change.

In the following examples I will try to convey the complexity and the significance of ending a consultancy project for the client and for the consultant.

One night stand

When I was asked to consult to the prop department of an opera house in Europe I felt the anthropological exhilaration of entering uncharted territory.

The work of the props was described as the kitchen of the organization. The makers prepared beautiful and complex objects on a very tight schedule in a highly pressurized environment; they concentrated on their products, loved working independently – and ignored everything else.

The department had a reputation for being difficult and unfriendly, both inside and outside the organization. Recent incidents among staff and complaints about stress levels had initiated the request for consultancy, but it was an ambivalent request: Leo, the head of department, wanted a quick fix – mainly some help to 'tell his staff off'. I managed to convince him of the need to interview people individually first, in order to gain some trust and build a broader picture of the organizational dynamics. We then organized a couple of workshops to address the difficulties among team members and to model a more cooperative, friendly and open way of working together. Despite Leo's scepticism and anxiety, the workshops went well and people seemed to use this opportunity to make some shifts in their approach and understanding of each other. However, Leo was in a rush to move on and put the negative experiences behind him. Despite my many attempts to continue the work with him and his deputy we never met again.

I wondered afterwards if my intervention was enough and if the shifts in behaviour and teamwork could be sustained. I also wondered if my attempts to continue the consultancy were connected to my unfulfilled desire – my experience of a 'one night stand' rather than a more in-depth relationship – and my ambition of influencing such an interesting and prestigious organization.

Waiting for Godot

Clarkson, the business division of a large non-profit organization, had survived numerous changes and traumatic events. It was now enjoying a new positive phase of stability and growth. The hopes and aspirations kept at bay for a number of years could now take to the wing. The management group in particular felt an increased pressure and desire to make innovative changes, to expand and create new opportunities for the centre. However, this wish to be more outward looking and to engage in new ventures did not fit with the fragility experienced within the division, the fear of radical changes felt by many staff members and their suspicions about the senior management of the wider system.

When we first met, the management group explained they had reached a still point, a sense of boredom and disillusion, very much in contrast with a previous stage when they had been able to rescue their organization from a near closure. After only a couple of sessions this torpor and stillness disappeared: the staff were able to resume old projects and make them come alive again; in particular, an extension to their building, which had been delayed for a long time, was now being built. However, a few months later the management group started to become increasingly annoyed with the senior management and began to develop a very radical and unrealistic plan: their independence from headquarters. Whereas they had regained some energy through their initial consultancy with me and things had started to develop again, now some of their grandiose fantasies, such as separating from headquarters, were killed off during our sessions together.

We agreed there was still work to be done together, yet I was left waiting: appointments were postponed and nobody seemed to want to close or acknowledge the need for a clear ending. I felt like the mother of an adolescent who had left home but who was still expecting his mother to be constantly available.

Clarkson left me in the dark about their intentions. During my subsequent telephone calls with them they always expressed an interest in continuing the consultancy, but they never did. Their power was expressed in keeping me waiting. During the consultancy I was experienced as both powerful when things started to develop again, and frustrating when I was unable to help the management group realize their dream of independence from headquarters.

By the end of the consultancy the management group of Clarkson had become more aware of their wish to avoid confronting the limits of their positions and the illusion that everything could be changed and re-shaped. Nevertheless, they have not been in touch – and I am still waiting!

A 'good enough' consultancy?

The consultancy may not be completed, but may be enough for now. A consultant needs to develop the ability to be content with the work that has been done.

It is tempting to think that we can have a major influence on all the organizations we work with. As a consequence, we may find it difficult to be satisfied with modest results. It can become a constant struggle to manage the ambitions one has for oneself and for the organization in a context where change and development are often very difficult to achieve. It requires flexibility and capacity to adapt to changing circumstances.

For example, during the first session of a new consultancy assignment, the manager, who had wanted the consultancy for his training department and negotiated for it, announced he was leaving. The consultancy was obviously doomed from the start: people reluctantly turned up at the first two sessions and then quit all together. But another member of staff, who had taken over the role of my original contact, saw the disruptiveness of the situation. She initially felt guilty towards me because of what had happened and accepted my offer to see her individually to continue the work. The result was a very constructive outcome: she was able to address difficult issues about her role and link her learning and insights back into the department.

Murder

Being sacked raises a number of questions. What did I miss? Did I do something wrong? What did I do wrong? Or what is wrong with them?

An abrupt or unsatisfactory ending reflects our limited capacity and the complexities of the organization we consult to. One-sided rejection can also be related to envy: the organization might deprive itself of the consultancy in order to prevent the consultant doing too good a job.

Millfield was a very deprived team: a sort of outpost for ethnic minorities with mental health problems, and part of a large health trust. My arrival was initially perceived as 'too good to be true', but soon hopelessness and despair re-emerged. A few months after my arrival, their health trust announced a plan to integrate the team with social services: this move was experienced as an additional problem, rather than something that could ease and complement their work.

They were already working in cramped conditions in a crumbling building: they could not imagine how they could accommodate other staff in that context. The consultancy sessions, which had been difficult but quite lively and animated, started losing their edge. Their manager attended very irregularly; she was busy in the trust negotiating the integration with social services. The team seemed to find it impossible to sustain a constructive relationship with me, as I represented the outside and western worlds. I was sacked, with no notice and no clear reason, only two months before the end of my contract.

To mark the ending of my assignment and in the hope of creating a bridge and an opening for the future, I wrote a letter to the manager saying: 'Abrupt endings are not healthy: they deprive the individuals and the team of understanding, of saying goodbye and of a more mature way of negotiating and taking a decision.' I felt quite humiliated and angry that they could not bear to wait until the end of the contract, that they wanted to leave everything unfinished and not worked through.

By coincidence, a wall outside their premises had been knocked down by a lorry months before I started. Shortly after my arrival the wall was rebuilt – but only in part. It was never completed. I kept reminding them that they could try to do something about their situation, including their physical environment. At first, the rebuilding of the wall seemed a sign of their wish to engage with me, and to move on; but perhaps I paid too little attention to the emotional 'broken wall', to their situation as a forgotten and bruised team. As a result, they made me powerless, blocking any possibility for me to have any further impact on their organization.

I wondered if they ever trusted me: the difference in our cultures and my 'proactive' role had a positive effect at the beginning, but it could not be sustained. My sense afterwards was that I missed something: I did not see or want to see their depression and pervasive feeling of isolation. At some level, they picked up on my ambivalence and my reluctance to stay with their despair. Maybe, very similarly to many well-meaning western organizations, I had wanted to help 'a developing country' do something about its situation, yet I did not relate enough to its grief. My wellbeing and my constructive approach also contributed to the abrupt ending. It was too much to bear: there was an unconscious wish to prevent me from being effective and successful.

A year later, Millfield's manager rang me up to ask if I could suggest a new consultant for the team. I was surprised, but also reassured, that my letter and my determination not to let them off the hook too easily had achieved a delayed positive outcome. The team went on working with a colleague: together they were able to work on important organizational issues.

Sometimes, the impulse to break off is closely related to the perception of the organization as 'terminally ill', or in a chronic state with no room for movement and change: this happens when the 'ego' of the organization is too fragile to allow for proper thinking and reflection to take place, and when the pain and distress of the staff are uncontained due to, in most cases, a lack of skilled management. The scope for consultancy then becomes very limited.

Contamination

Orange House was a children's home where the team found out that a member of staff had developed a very close relationship with one of the girls in its care. Suspicions started to emerge about the nature of their relationship, and there was a widespread fear that staff and management might have been deceived for many months. The team was shocked: the staff member involved had been criticized before about his approach to work and his radical ideas, but nothing improper had previously been suggested, let alone abusive behaviour. There was a growing sense of shame and a strong desire to blame someone for what had happened. Trust had been broken: the team now felt traumatized by the whole experience.

I had a key role in raising the alarm, yet a few months later I was made 'redundant'. The official reason given was that there was no more funding. My experience was that I was perceived as 'contaminated' by what had happened, and held responsible for not having been able to prevent it. My understanding now is that the ending of my consultancy was strongly related to the unconscious need to 'clean up' the organization – a sort of organizational purging. The hope was that some of the pain and shame of what had happened would disappear with me.

During my work with Orange House I was often on the verge of giving it up. Many managers came and did not stay: nobody seemed to want or be able to survive this unit. Yet I felt I could not leave until the team reached some stability. This situation fuelled my omnipotent fantasies of being indispensable and central to the team. Undoubtedly, this fantasy also helped me to stay.

In the last session, Robyn, an administrator who had been around for a long time, said that she associated me with a number of difficult events in the history of Orange House: she wished I could take them away with me. Someone else compared me with an over-possessive parent who did not want to let go, while another staff member said, 'There is a time when you have to leave home.' However, towards the end of the session another member of staff wondered if it was safe to let me go – had they taken the right decision?

In the past years I had survived and resisted numerous attempts to 'throw me out'. This time it felt different and I let it happen. Part of me was very relieved to leave the 'contaminated' field. It had been a major challenge consulting to Orange House, helping the staff to survive many crises and a very absent management. Only in the last two years of my consultancy had the unit reached some stability thanks to a competent manager who was able to endure the tempestuous situation. I had been acting as the memory of the group as well as one of the more stable influences. I felt tired and worn out. But I also felt that they had not fully recognized my input, my resilience and my contribution to their survival. I could not help thinking that at the end of the day they had the power to get rid of me.

However, for the first time the team was capable of dealing with the process of leaving in an open and constructive way, acknowledging their feelings of resentment, guilt, relief and loss: they were able to address some of the reasons behind the ending and to say goodbye in a more informed and mature way. A few years on, the organization has survived and now has a new manager, a former staff member who has come back to Orange House after further training and management experience in another unit.

Letting go

Ian, the owner of a small business, had been my client for several years. I started coaching him when he was still employed in an organization where he had become increasingly unhappy. He had a difficult relationship with his boss, whom he perceived as being judgemental and unsympathetic. He felt he couldn't develop in the organization and needed to leave.

It was a painful process. He had invested a lot in the organization and felt very angry and resentful about what had happened. However, being young and talented, Ian was ready to move on and develop his own business. He started a consultancy company that grew very quickly and he was able to develop interesting new ventures.

My role was to help him to reflect on particularly difficult assignments, to develop his business model and to think about his management role with his associates. We developed a strong collaborative relationship and I looked forward to the sessions with him. He always came with plenty to discuss – sometimes involving very demanding situations relating to clients or associates. I found the material both challenging and stimulating.

This assignment started when I was still mostly working part-time in my career: I identified with Ian and felt at times vicariously proud of his successes. I was also occasionally jealous of his opportunities and envious of his entrepreneurial skills, which I felt I didn't have. However, during the last couple of years of our work together, Ian became increasingly interested in a more personal and spiritual journey; his focus on developing his business became secondary and he started to consider a different career path. I gradually became aware of a shift in my role and perspective, realizing that my contribution to his thinking and development was becoming less relevant and that most of his new ideas were being generated outside the sessions. However, after many years of working together, it was difficult to let go and acknowledge the changes.

When I finally raised the issue of a possible ending, Ian told me that he had had exactly the same thought earlier in the session, but had been unable to articulate it. We were both struggling to let go of a relationship that had worked well and which had given us new learning opportunities and pleasure.

Afterwards, I did wonder whether we should have stopped earlier. Perhaps we were both embroiled in our mutual dependency, our loyalty to each other and fear of separation. Many of Ian's changes coincided with his move to a new house a couple of years earlier. The change of house became the catalyst for a 'new life' personally and professionally. And I represented the parental home that it was difficult to leave – or which needed to be there, just in case.

As Peter Marris points out, the essential bridge between social and psychological aspects of human behaviour is attachment:

> We each create our own meaning out of a unique experience of attachment which is still also recognizably the product of a culture.
>
> (Marris, 1991, p. 88)

> While attachment and dependency are linked – children depend on their attachment figures and as adults we also usually channel our personal dependency needs on our attachment figures – there are important differences between them. Attachment, unlike dependency, requires specificity and proximity.... Attachment provides us with the security needed for independence and exploration. Having our dependency needs met, on the other hand, does not equip us for this; in fact remaining overly dependent, inhibits exploration.
>
> (Braun, 2011, p. 12)

The tension between dependency and attachment is also found in the consultant. Dependency is linked to the fear of becoming redundant and insignificant, the unconscious primitive terror of annihilation while the client is moving on to greater things. A fear of separation makes it more difficult to keep the end in view and to plan for it. And naturally our capacity to separate is affected by other significant separations.

The attachment is both to the client and to the work. It is particularly difficult to let go of something we have contributed to in a substantial way and to say goodbye to someone with whom we have developed a close relationship. Inevitably there is a parallel with the experience of letting one's young adult children go.

It is challenging to give up our desire to be indispensable and acknowledge our clients' capacity – and wish – to move on.

The psychological necessity of mourning

> … the management of change and organizational transitions depends upon our ability to articulate the process of grieving.
>
> (Marris, 1993, p. 91)

Our wish to move on, to introduce changes and to create new beginnings can compromise our ability to deal with closure and ending. The challenge is to work through this process without losing our capacity for hope and desire.

When an ending and the feelings associated with it are recognized we can move on to a more fluid state of transition, a paradoxical stage:

> at the edge of chaos, in which behaviour is both stable enough for the system not to fall apart and unstable enough not to get stuck in one pattern…. It is a position where there is excitement, tension, but also anxiety.
>
> (Stacey, 1997, p. 187)

Today, the continual changes and transitions experienced by many organizations force their staff and managements to deal with constant endings and new beginnings. Often very little attention is paid to these processes and to the need for organizational mourning and grief. It seems there is no time to pause and take stock: organizations are expected to move on faster and faster and to adjust very quickly. Our society values movement, energy and fitness. On the other hand, through the media, we are regularly exposed to death and catastrophe in a detached and dramatic way. However, it is these ordinary, everyday deaths and losses that are not given enough space in our personal and organizational life.

Endings are never easy. As consultants, when we are able to be open to our own vulnerability and conflicting feelings we have a better chance of helping our client organizations address their 'ordinary' endings in ways that are meaningful to them.

Conclusion

In the journey of writing this book, I have encountered moments of deep frustration and of surprising reward. In times of coexisting and conflicting feelings, Winnicott's 'good enough' concept has been a key guiding principle.

Developing my thoughts and revisiting my work has enabled me to connect with the texture of what I do, learning and relearning anew. The challenge has been to convey key ideas, experiences and dynamics that could resonate with the readership in my mind: people at work, organizational leaders, students of organizational consultancy and my colleagues. I hope they will find this book accessible and helpful.

I also hope my writing has contributed to the development of a discipline still '*in fieri*', and helps to generate curiosity and interest in this field. Given its inherent back stage character, the craft and practice of the organizational consultancy approach is not always easy to capture.

It is the stories I tell that are the bones of this book. Through the examples they contain, I try to convey the complexity of the world of work today: the personal and organizational cost of ill-conceived organizational structures and tasks, as well as the creativity and positive energy that work can generate.

This book is also an account of my own personal work journey and the challenges I have faced in my development as an organisational consultant. Opening myself to the experiences of my clients, responding to unexpected dynamics and situations, and at times being recipient of negative projections has not been easy. I have had to learn how to understand the meaning of what was happening, while maintaining a level of focus without feeling too overwhelmed or personally challenged. I have also felt incredibly touched by people's stories and by their capacity to develop, in spite of organizational ordeals and complex early life experiences. Witnessing positive organizational change is still a great motivation to continue being involved in this area of work.

'The team in my mind' are the colleagues I first met when I was a trainee at Tavistock Institute, and the new colleagues I encountered over the years in connection with my work with Tavistock Consulting. They remain a source of great support and inspiration. Engaging and listening to their consultancy work, and sharing my own experiences of challenging assignments have been essential ingredients that, I hope, have allowed me to provide my present and past clients with a consultancy that has been 'good enough'.

Bibliography

Alford, C. F. (2001) 'Leadership by Interpretation and Holding', *Organisational and Social Dynamics*, No 2: 153–173.

Amado, G. and Ambrose, A. (2001) *The Transitional Approach to Change*. London: Karnac.

Amado, G. (2009) 'Potential space: the threatened source of individual and collective creativity', in Sievers, B. (ed.), *Psychoanalytic Studies of Organizations*. London: Karnac.

Armstrong, D. (1999) 'The recovery of meaning' in French, R. and Vince, R. (eds), *Group Relations, Management and Organization*. Oxford University Press

Armstrong, D. (2005) *Organization in the Mind*. London: Karnac.

Armstrong, D. (2007) 'The dynamics of Lateral Relations in Changing Organizational Worlds', *Organisational and Social Dynamics*, Vol 7, No 2: 193–210.

Armstrong, D. and Rustin, M. (2015) *Social Defences against Anxiety. Explorations in a Paradigm*. London: Karnac.

Ball, S. (2003) 'The teacher's soul and the terrors of performativity', *Journal of Education Policy*, Vol 18, No 2: 215–228.

Bauman, Z. (2000) *Liquid Modernity*. Cambridge: Polity Press.

Bazalgette, J. L., Irvine, G. B. and Quine, C. (2009) *The Purpose of Meaning and the Meaning of Purpose: A Container for our Atomized yet Globalised World*. ISPSO, Toledo, Spain.

Bick, E. (1968) 'The experience of the skin in early object relations', *International Journal of Psychoanalysis*, 49: 484–486. Reprinted in: Briggs, A. *Surviving Space: Papers on Infant Observation*. London: Karnac, 2002.

Billington, M. (2013) 'The National theatre at 50: Michael Billington's view from the stalls', *Guardian*.

Bion, W. R. (1961) *Experiences in Groups and Other Papers*. London: Tavistock Publications.

Bion, W. R. (1963) *Elements of Psychoanalysis*. London: Heinemann; reprinted London: Karnac, 1984.

Bion, W. R. (1965) *Transformations: Change from Learning to Growth*. London: Heinemann; reprinted London: Karnac, 1984.

Bion, W. R. (1970) *Attention and Interpretation*. London: Tavistock Publications.

Bion, W. R. (1991) *A Memoir of the Future*. London: Karnac Books.

Bollas, C. (1987) *The Shadow of the Object: Psychoanalysis of the Unthought Known*. New York: Columbia University Press.

Bollas, C. (2000) 'Architecture and the Unconscious', *International Forum of Psychoanalysis*, 9: 28–42.

Bolton, W. and Cardona, F. (2004) *Invitation to Collude: The Complexity of Engagement between Client and Consultant*. Unpublished paper.

Bowlby, J. (1961) 'Process of mourning', *International Journal of Psychoanalysis vol. XLII*.

Bowlby, J. (1969) *Attachment and Loss Volume 1. Attachment*. London: Hogarth Press and the Institute of Psychoanalysis. Reprinted 1997, London: Pimlico.

Bowlby, J. (1973) *Attachment Theory, Separation Anxiety and Mourning*. London: Tavistock Clinic.

Braun, G. (2011) 'Organizations today: *what* happens to attachment?', *Psychodynamic Practice*, Vol 17, No 2, May 2011.

Britton, R. (1989) 'The missing link: Parental Sexuality in the Oedipus complex'. In: *The Oedipus Complex Today: Clinical Implications*. London: Karnac.

Britton, R. (1992) 'The Oedipus situation and the depressive position', in Anderson, R. *Clinical Lectures on Klein and Bion*, London: Routledge.

Britton, R. (2003) *Sex, Death and the Superego. Experiences in Psychoanalysis*, London: Karnac.

Britton, R. (2004) 'Subjectivity, Objectivity, and Triangular Space (2004)', *Psychoanalytic Quarterly*, 73: 47–61.

Broucek, F. J. (1991) *Shame and the Self*. The Guilford Press, New York.

Brunod, M. (2002) 'Le organizzazioni nell'era postmoderna fra trasparenze e occultamenti', *Spunti* n.5 . Milano: Studio APS Analisi Psicosociologica.

Cardona, F. (1994a) 'Uncovering and Thinking about Organisational Secrets', *What makes consultancy work – understanding the dynamics. Proceedings of the International Consulting Conference*, London: South Bank University Press.

Cardona, F. (1994b) 'Facing an uncertain future', in Obholzer, A. and Roberts, V. (eds), *The Unconscious at Work*, London: Routledge.

Cardona, F. and Raffaelli, D. (2016) 'Turbulent Family and Organisational Dynamics in the Context of Succession in a Family Business: A Joint Intervention to Contain and Work through Destructive Oedipal Forces', *Organisational and Social Dynamics*, Vol. 16 (2) 245–254.

Cardona, F. and Damon, S. (2019) 'Family patterns at work: how casting light on the shadows of the past can enhance leadership in the present', in Obholzer, A. and Roberts, V. (eds), *The Unconscious at Work*, second edition. London: Routledge.

Carr, W. (2001) 'The Exercise of Authority in a Dependent Context', in Gould, L., Stapley L. F. and Stein, M. (eds), *The Systems Psychodynamics of Organizations*. London: Karnac.

Coles, P. (2003) *The Importance of Sibling Relations in Psychoanalysis*. London: Karnac.

Conan Doyle, A. (2015) *The Adventure of the Cardboard Box*. Shepperd Publication.

Cooper, A. and Dartington, T. (2004) 'The vanishing organisation: organisational containment in a networked world', in Huffington, C. and Armstrong, D. (eds), *Working Below the Surface*. London: Karnac.

Copley, B. (1993) *The World of Adolescence. Literature, Society and Psychoanalytic Psychotherapy*. London: Free Association Books.

Danze, E. A. (2005) 'An Architect's View of Introspective Space: the analytic Vessel', *Annals of Psychoanalysis*, 33: 109–124.

Dartington, T. (2010) *Managing Vulnerability The Underlying Dynamics of Systems of Care*. London: Karnac.

de Botton, A. (2009) *The Pleasures and Sorrows of Work*. New York: Vintage Books.

Donne, J. (2012) *The Best of John Donne*. Create Space Independent Publishing Platform.

Erikson, E. H. (1959) 'Identity and the Life Cycle', *Psychological Issues*, 1/1: 1–171.

Erlich, H. S. (2001) 'Enemies within and without: Paranoia and regression in groups and organizations', in Gould, L., Stapley L. F. and Stein, M. (eds), *The Systems Psychodynamics of Organizations*. London: Karnac.

Foster, A. (2001) 'The duty to care and the need to split', *Journal of Social Work Practice*, 15(1), 81–90.

French, R. and Simpson, P. (2001) 'Learning at the Edges between Knowing and not Knowing: "Translating" Bion', *Organisational and Social Dynamics*, 1(1), 54–77.

Freud, S. (1917) 'Mourning and Melancholia' in *Collected Papers*, Vol. 4, London: Hogarth Press, 1925.

Freud, S. (1920) *Beyond the Pleasure Principle*. London: Penguin, 2003.

Garland, C. (2004) *Understanding Trauma*. London: Karnac.

Gould, L. (2010) 'Barack Obama's post partisan dream: leadership and the limits of the depressive position', in Brunning, H. and Perini, M. (eds), *Psychoanalytic Perspectives on a Turbulent World*. London: Karnac.

Halton, W. (2004) 'By what authority? Psychoanalytical reflections on creativity and Change in relation to organizational life', in Huffington, C. and Armstrong, D. (eds), *Working Below the Surface*. London: Karnac.

Halton, W. (2011) Private communication.

Hirschhorn, L. (1988) *The Workplace Within: Psychodynamics of Organisational Life*. Cambridge, MA: MIT Press.

Hirschhorn, L. (1997) *Reworking Authority: Leading and Following in the Post-Modern Organisation*. Cambridge, Massachusetts, London: The MIT Press.

Hirschhorn, L. (1999) 'The Primary Risk', *Human Relations*, Vol. 52, No 1: 1–154.

Hirschhorn, L. and Horowitz, S. (2015) 'Extreme work environments: beyond anxiety and social defence', in *Social Defences against Anxiety. Explorations in a Paradigm*. London: Karnac.

Hoggett, P. (2016) Tavistock Lecture, *'Shame and Performativity: Thoughts on the Psychology of Neo-liberalism'*.

Hoggett, P. (2017) OPUS Lecture, *'Shame in Organisations'*.

Huffington, C. (2004) 'What women leaders can tell us', in Huffington, C. and Armstrong, D. (eds), *Working Below the Surface*. London: Karnac.

Hughes, L. and Pengelly, P. (1997) *Staff Supervision in a Turbulent Environment*. London: Jessica Kingsley.

Hunt, J. M. (2000) *Organizational Leadership and Shame*, ISPSO.

Izod, K. (2016) 'Representation, place and equivalent realities; an exploration of relational perspectives on representations and meaning', *Organisational and Social Dynamics*, Vol. 16 (1) 110–128.

Jaques, E. (1955) 'Social systems as a defence against persecutory and depressive anxiety', in Klein, M., Heimann, P. and Money-Kyrle, R. E. (eds), *New Directions in Psychoanalysis*. London: Tavistock Publications: reprinted London: Karnac, 1985.

Jaques, E. (1965) 'Death and the middle-life crises', in Spillius, E. B. (ed.), *Melanie Klein Today, Volume 2: Mainly Practice*, London: Routledge, 1990.

Kahn, W. A. (1992) 'To be fully there: psychological presence at work', *Human Relations*, 45: 321–350.

Karpman, S. (1968) 'Fairy Tales and Script Drama Analysis', *Transactional Analysis Bulletin*, 7, 26.

Keats, J. (1817) *The Letters of John Keats*. Oxford: Oxford University Press, 1952.

Kets de Vries, M. F. R. (2009) *Reflections on Character and Leadership*. Jossey-Bass A Wiley Imprint.

Klein, M. (1959) 'Our adult world and its roots in infancy', lecture at the University of Manchester, in Colman, A. D. and Geller, M. H. (eds), *Group Relations Reader 2*, A. K. Rice Institute Series [Washington, DC], 1985.

Klein, M. (1975) *Collected Works, Vol. 3*. London: Hogarth Press.

Krantz, J. (2001) 'Dilemmas of Organisational change: A systemic Psychoadynamic perspective', in Gould, L., Stapley, L. F. and Stein, M. (eds), *The Systems Psychodynamics of Organizations*. London: Karnac.

Krantz, J. (2015) 'Social defences in the information age', in *Social Defences against Anxiety. Explorations in a Paradigm*. London: Karnac.

Lanzara, G. (1993) *Capacita' Negativa*. Bologna: Il Mulino.

Lawrence, G. (1999) 'A mind for business', in French, R. and Vince, R. (eds), *Group Relations, Management and Organization*. Oxford: Oxford University Press.

Levy, S. and Lemma, A. (2004) *The Perversion of Loss. Psychoanalytic Perspectives on Trauma*. Whurr Publishers, London.

Lohmer, M. and Lazar, R. A. (2006) 'The consultant between the lines of fire: the dynamics of trust, mistrust and containment in organisations', *Organisational and Social Dynamics*, 6(1): 42–62.

Long, S. (2015) 'Beyond Identifying Social Defences: "working through" and lessons from people whispering', in Armstrong, D. (ed.), *Social Defences against Anxiety: Explorations in a Paradigm*. London: Routledge.

Lucey, A. (2015) 'Corporate culture and inner conflicts', in Armstrong, D. and Rustin, M. (eds), *Social Defences against Anxiety. Explorations in a Paradigm*. London: Karnac.

Manzo, L. C. and Devine-Wright, P. (eds) (2014) *Place Attachment, Advances in Theory, Methods and Application*. London: Routledge.

Marris, P. (1991) 'The Social Construction of Uncertainty', in Parkes, C. M., Stevenson-Hinde, J. and Marris, P. (eds), *Attachment across the Life Cycle*. London and New York: Routledge.

Marris, P. (1993) *Loss and Change*. London: Routledge.

Marris, P. (1996) *The Politics of Uncertainty: Attachment in Private and Public Life*. London, Routledge.

Mattinson, J. (1992) *The Reflection Process in Casework Supervision*. London: Tavistock Institute of Marital studies 1975; second edition.

Menninger, K. A. (1942) *Love against Hate*. New York: Harcourt Brace.

Menzies Lyth, I. (1988) *Containing Anxieties in Institutions: Selected Essays*. London: Free Association Books.

Menzies Lyth, I. (1989) *The Dynamics of the Social: Selected Essays*. London: Free Association Books.

Miller, E. J. and Rice, A. K. (1967) *Systems of Organizations: The Control of Task and Sentient Boundaries*. London: Tavistock Publications (reprinted, Routledge, 2001).

Miller, E. J. and Gwynne, G. (1972) *A Life a Part*. London: Tavistock Publications.

Miller, E. J. (1993) *From Dependency to Autonomy*. London: Free Association Books.

Miller, E. J. (1999) 'Dependency, alienation or partnership? The changing relatedness of the individual to the enterprise', in French and Vince (eds), *Group Relations Management and Organisation*. Oxford: Oxford University Press.

Mitchell, J. (2014) 'Siblings and the psychosocial', *Organisational and Social Dynamics*, 14(1): 1–12.

Morgan, G. (1986) *Images of Organisations*. London: Sage Publications.

Murdin, L. (2000) *How Much is Enough? Endings in Psychotherapy and Counselling.* London: Routledge.

Neumann, J. (1994) 'Difficult beginnings, confrontation between client and consultant', in Casemore, R. (ed.), *What Makes Consultancy Work – Understanding the Dynamics. Proceedings of the International Consulting Conference, 1994.* London: South Bank University Press, pp. 13–47.

Obholzer, A. (2001) 'The leader, the unconscious and the management of the organization', in Gould, L., Stapley, L. F. and Stein, M. (eds), *The Systems Psychodynamics of Organizations.* London: Karnac.

Obholzer, A. (2003) 'Some reflections on concepts of relevance to Consulting and also to the management of Organisations', *Organisational and Social Dynamics*, Volume 3 No. 1.

Obholzer, A. (2019) 'Authority power and leadership: contributions from group relations training', in Obholzer, A. and Roberts, V. (eds), *The Unconscious at Work.* London: Routledge.

Osnes, G. (2014) 'Succession as Strategic Space in Family Capitalism: A Founder of Third Generation Succession Case Explored', *Organisational and Social Dynamics*, 14(1): 76–101.

Pallasmaa, J. U. (1994) 'An Architecture of the Seven Senses', in Holl, S., Pallasmaa, J. and Perez Gomez, A. (eds), *Questions of Perception, Phenomenology of Architecture*, pp. 27–38. San Francisco, CA: William Stout.

Parkes, C. M. (1996) *Bereavement Studies of Grief in Adult Life.* London: Routledge.

Pinker, S. (2008) *The Sexual Paradox.* London: Atlantic Books.

Roberts, V. Z. (2005) 'Birth and bereavement: the emotional impact of organizational change'. Keynote paper given at New Directions Conference 'Psychoanalysis and Group Process', Washington D.C., 11–13 February.

Sandler, A. M. (1977) 'Beyond eight month anxiety', *International Journal of Psycho-Analysis*, 58: 195–207.

Schinaia, C. (2016) *Psychoanalysis and Architecture, The Inside and the Outside.* London: Karnac.

Schultz, A. (1944) 'The Stranger: an essay in social psychology', *American Journal of Sociology*, 49: 499–507.

Sennett, R. (1998) *The Corrosion of Character: The Personal Consequences of Work in the New Capitalism.* New York: Norton.

Sievers, B. (2009) 'Against All reason: Trusting in Trust', in Sievers, B. (ed.), *Psychoanalytic Studies of Organizations.* London: Karnac.

Silverstone, J. (2006) 'Siblings', in Coles, P., *Sibling Relationships.* London: Karnac.

Stacey, R. (1997) 'Excitement and tension at the edge of chaos', in Smith, E. (ed.), *Integrity and Change.* London: Routledge.

Stacey, R. (2001) 'Complexity at the "Edge" of the Basic-Assumption Group', in Gould, L., Stapley, L. F. and Stein, M. (eds), *The Systems Psychodynamics of Organizations.* London: Karnac.

Steiner, J. (1985) 'Turning a blind eye: the cover up for Oedipus'. *International Review of Psycho-Analysis*, 12, (2), 161–172.

Steiner J. (2006) 'Seeing and Being Seen: Narcissistic Pride and Narcissistic Humiliation', *International Journal of Psychoanalysis*, 87, 939–951.

Stokes, J. (2019) 'Institutional chaos and personal stress', in Obholzer, A. and Roberts, V. (eds), *The Unconscious at Work*, second edition. London: Routledge.

Walker, M. (1997) 'Working with abused clients in an institutional setting', in Smith, E. (ed.), *Integrity and Change*. London: Routledge.

Winnicott, D. W. (1958) 'Hate in the counter-transference' (1947), in Winnicott, D., *Collected Papers: Through Paediatrics to Psycho-analysis*. London: Tavistock Publications.

Winnicott, D. W. (1969) 'Adolescent Process and the Need for Personal Confrontation', *Pediatrics*, Vol 44, part 1.

Winnicott, D. W. (1971) *Playing and Reality*. London: Tavistock Publications (Reprinted Harmondsworth: Penguin Books, 1980).

Yeats, W. B. (1919) 'The second coming', in Harmon, W. (ed.), *The Classic Hundred Poems*. New York: Columbia University Press, 1998.

Index

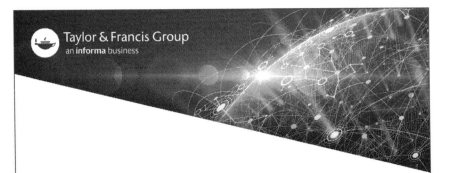

Printed in Great Britain
by Amazon